CONCEPTUAL PLAYWORLDS FOR WELLBEING

This vital resource uses the evidence-driven Conceptual PlayWorlds model of intentional teaching developed by Professor Marilyn Fleer to provide supporting classroom or home-based activities to help children aged between four and eight solve challenges and learn wellbeing concepts through play.

Intended for use with the accompanying picture story book, *The Lonely Little Cactus*, a tale about a cactus that feels lonely living in the desert, this guide offers imagery-rich scenarios, including 20 unique activities, so children have an opportunity to experientially grasp wellbeing concepts that can be otherwise difficult to explain. This resource guides educators and teachers through a range of wellbeing activities, including:

- Identifying feelings

- Coping (social support, problem solving, and self-regulation)

- Friendships (relationship building, working together, time with friends, social skills)

- Positive emotions (happiness, joy, doing something you love, enjoyment, fun)

- Relaxation strategies

- Belonging and inclusion (working together, collaboration, joining in play, including others)

Offering a unique opportunity for children to learn about psychological strategies while being engaged in a beautiful narrative and visually captivating illustrations, this is the ideal resource for educators or teachers, support staff, practitioners, and families looking to help children understand and manage their feelings. While the context is centre-based, the activities can be done almost anywhere, such as in family homes, the Botanical Gardens, when on holidays, or when visiting a park.

Kelly-Ann Allen is an associate professor, educational and developmental psychologist, and belonging researcher at Monash University. You can find Kelly-Ann on Twitter, Instagram, and Facebook @drkellyallen. Resources for wellbeing and belonging can be found at *www.drkellyallen.com*.

Marilyn Fleer is an Australian Research Council Laureate Fellow and holds the foundation chair in early childhood education and development at Monash University. She researches in the areas of early childhood science, engineering, and technologies with particular attention on digital visual methodology framed through cultural-historical theory. @MarilynFleer is on Twitter and Facebook.

Lara McKinley is an award-winning content producer and communications manager at Monash University. Lara partners with researchers to translate their work to maximise engagement and impact. You can find Lara online on Twitter @Lara_McKinley and LinkedIn and via her website, *www.laramckinley.com*.

CONCEPTUAL PLAYWORLDS FOR WELLBEING

A RESOURCE BOOK FOR THE LONELY LITTLE CACTUS

Kelly-Ann Allen, Marilyn Fleer and Lara McKinley

Routledge
Taylor & Francis Group

LONDON AND NEW YORK

Designed cover image: © Madeleine Griffith

First published 2024
by Routledge
4 Park Square, Milton Park, Abingdon, Oxon OX14 4RN

and by Routledge
605 Third Avenue, New York, NY 10158

Routledge is an imprint of the Taylor & Francis Group, an informa business

Text: © 2024 Kelly-Ann Allen, Marilyn Fleer and Lara McKinley

Illustrations: © Madeleine Griffith

British Library Cataloguing-in-Publication Data
A catalogue record for this book is available from the British Library

ISBN: 978-1-032-07365-1 (pbk)
ISBN: 978-1-003-20656-9 (ebk)

DOI: 10.4324/9781003206569

Typeset in Din
by Apex CoVantage, LLC

CONTENTS

ACKNOWLEDGEMENTS

We would like to take this opportunity to acknowledge Dr Prabhat Rai and thank the Australian Research Council for supporting the original research (DP130101438; DP140101131; LP150100279). We would also like to thank the Laureate Fellowship grant from the Australian Research Council (FL180100161) for giving time to Marilyn Fleer for the important translation work needed to bring the research into a new conceptual area of wellbeing. Translation of research to support educators and teachers with the planning of their programs in early childhood settings is a key outcome for all researchers and is a highly valued aim of the grant awarded 2018–2024.

ABOUT THE CONTRIBUTORS

Kelly-Ann Allen, PhD FAPS, is an associate professor and educational and developmental psychologist in the School of Educational Psychology and Counselling, Faculty of Education, Monash University, and a Principal Honorary Fellow at the Centre for Wellbeing Science, University of Melbourne. She is also the co-director and founder of the Global Belonging Collaborative, which represents a consortium of belonging researchers and advocates from around the world. Dr Allen is the editor-in-chief of the *Educational and Developmental Psychologist,* and both the current and founding co-editor-in-chief of the *Journal of Belonging and Human Connection*. Dr Allen's work is characterised by accessible applications of her research into everyday practice, especially as it relates to the core beneficiaries of the work. You can find Kelly-Ann on Twitter, Instagram, and Facebook @drkellyallen. Resources for wellbeing and belonging can be found at www.drkellyallen.com.

Marilyn Fleer, PhD, holds the Foundation Chair in Early Childhood Education and Development at Monash University, where she is also a Kathleen Fitzpatrick Australian Laureate Fellow. She researches in the areas of early childhood science, engineering, and technologies with particular attention on digital visual methodology framed through cultural-historical theory. Her Laureate Fellowship on the theme "Imagination in play and imagination in STEM" investigates how families and teachers create conditions for children's conceptual thinking in play-based settings. She has published widely in international journals including *Mind*; *Culture and Activity*; *Research in Science Education*; *Learning, Culture and Social Interaction*; and *Cultural Studies of Science Education*. She founded the *International Journal of Research in Early Childhood*, which is an open-access journal designed to support scholarship in early childhood education research. @MarilynFleer is on Twitter and Facebook.

Lara McKinley is an award-winning content producer and communications manager at Monash University. She is passionate about research translation and using communications strategies to support researchers to create long-term impact with their work. Lara started her career as a photojournalist, covering stories in Guatemala, Timor-Leste, the US, and Australia, and later worked as a visual storyteller in international development. Lara's work has been broadcast nationally and internationally on television, radio, print, and online. Outside her work at Monash, Lara partners with organisations to produce content strategies, visual stories, and story-based content that builds connection, increases engagement, and creates change. You can find Lara online on Twitter @lara_mckinley and LinkedIn and via her website: www.laramckinley.com.

Chapter one

CONCEPTUAL PLAYWORLDS FOR WELLBEING

Conceptual PlayWorlds for Wellbeing: A Practical Resource for The Lonely Little Cactus offers an evidence-informed model of intentionality in play-based settings developed by Laureate Professor Marilyn Fleer at Monash University (Fleer, 2018). The Conceptual PlayWorlds approach focuses on children's play and stories as they learn wellbeing and coping concepts through *The Lonely Little Cactus: A Story About Friendship and Coping*.

The Lonely Little Cactus presents an engaging narrative of a cactus who struggles to make friends. He feels lonely and learns quickly that loneliness is not remedied by simply having others around. Before he can overcome his feelings of loneliness, he needs to cope with them. The little cactus discovers that not all coping skills are helpful and are, in fact, unique to the individual. What works for one person may not work for another. When he engages in a range of coping strategies (some more helpful than others), he finds a strategy that works. Moreover, in doing so, he makes a lifelong friend.

Creating *Conceptual PlayWorlds for Wellbeing* around *The Lonely Little Cactus* allows us to dive deep into wellbeing concepts with young children. All young children face daily challenges that require them to cope with stress. Some of these challenges may seem trivial to adults, but for young children, who are still learning to regulate their emotions, they can feel like big problems.

Young children need guidance and education to learn social and emotional competencies in the same way they require assistance to learn literacy and numeracy skills.

This book allows early childhood educators, teachers, and young children to enter the story of *The Lonely Little Cactus* through play and provides fun, enjoyable, experiential, and intentional moments with young children about managing emotions, coping with problems, and building wellbeing.

DOI: 10.4324/9781003206569-1

How to use this resource

A *Conceptual PlayWorld* is a teaching model that educators or teachers use to teach concepts to children through play. This resource details 20 Conceptual PlayWorlds for building wellbeing. Each Conceptual PlayWorld combines stories and imaginary play and presents problems that need to be solved. The Conceptual PlayWorlds bring children, educators, and teachers into an imaginary situation – not necessarily in the same way as the traditional educator or teacher-student relationship, but as play-partners going on adventures and solving problems together. Problem-solving is an essential element of wellbeing and learning. Therefore, Conceptual PlayWorlds for Wellbeing are designed to be play-based, inspiring children to research and solve any challenges that arise.

Conceptual PlayWorlds for Wellbeing are built around the story of *The Lonely Little Cactus* by Kelly-Ann Allen and illustrated by Madeleine Griffith. The Conceptual PlayWorlds for Wellbeing included in this resource create imaginary situations that can be collectively shared by all the children, educators, and teachers involved rather than individual children or groups of children creating their imaginary play. Conceptual PlayWorlds for Wellbeing is inclusive of all children because all children can quickly enter the play and become play partners. All children have an opportunity to engage in cooperative play.

In Conceptual PlayWorlds for Wellbeing, educators and teachers have a range of roles, such as being inside the play as play partners. They can lead play or they can follow the children's lead. Early childhood educators and teachers can also be with the children as equal play partners. They model the spirit of play, support the inclusion of all children, and encourage children to make positive contributions. The wellbeing concepts and play skills experienced in Conceptual PlayWorlds for Wellbeing can be transferred to other play scenarios. The Conceptual PlayWorlds for Wellbeing are designed to be:

1. Pop-ups for a brief period, such as during group time and free choice time
2. Long-term over a day, week, or even a term

Each Conceptual PlayWorld for Wellbeing in the resource details strategies and prompts that build wellbeing. The activities are inspired by research on relationship building, social and emotional competencies (such as coping skills and emotional regulation), positive psychology, and belonging research.

The authors bring together three unique areas of expertise. Associate Professor Dr Kelly-Ann Allen is an award-winning educational and developmental psychologist and author of *The Lonely Little Cactus*. Laureate Professor Marilyn Fleer is a former kindergarten teacher and is now a world-leading researcher who developed the Conceptual PlayWorld model. Lara

McKinley is a passionate advocate in research translation and communication. This book draws on their experience working with educators, teachers, parents, and young children. Each activity outlines steps for setting up and developing the play-based scenarios.

Every Conceptual PlayWorld for Wellbeing detailed in the book extends the story of *The Lonely Little Cactus*. The book may be used with children in a traditional story time fashion. However, once the story concludes, children have an opportunity to step into Conceptual PlayWorlds for Wellbeing and begin to explore the characters and problems in more detail. Conceptual PlayWorlds allow children to try out, first-hand, the wellbeing concepts touched on in the book and work with their class community to build their own wellbeing and coping strategies.

Why use *The Lonely Little Cactus* to explore Conceptual PlayWorlds for Wellbeing?

The Lonely Little Cactus is a book that explores coping and resilience in ways that build young children's understanding and agency. The main character in the book is the Lonely Little Cactus, who experiences loneliness. Through the characters he meets within the book – Bat, Deer, and Porcupine – he builds strategies that help him cope with his feelings. Little Cactus builds a small community, much like children in a classroom. The interactive way the characters interact to help Little Cactus serves as a model for children to help others within their class environment.

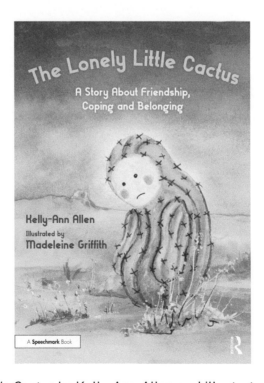

Figure 1.1 *The Lonely Little Cactus* by Kelly-Ann Allen and illustrated by Madeleine Griffith

A Conceptual PlayWorld has five characteristics (Fleer, 2018): 1. Selecting a story for the Conceptual PlayWorld, 2. Designing a Conceptual PlayWorld space, 3. Entering and exiting the Conceptual PlayWorld space, 4. Planning the play inquiry or problem scenario, and 5. Planning early childhood educators or teachers' interactions to build wellbeing. This is visually depicted in Figure 1.2 with details in Table 1.1.

The characteristics of a Conceptual PlayWorld that will be used in each Conceptual PlayWorlds for Wellbeing in this resource are described in the following section. The first step, selecting a story, has been done for this resource: *The Lonely Little Cactus*, written by Kelly-Ann Allen and illustrated by Madeleine Griffith.

 ## Designing a Conceptual PlayWorld for Wellbeing space

Planning for a particular space in the classroom or centre that becomes the imaginary situation is vital for signalling when the children are in the Conceptual PlayWorld for Wellbeing and when they are not. It is a space where all the children enter together as a

Figure 1.2 The five characteristics of a Conceptual PlayWorld (Fleer, 2018)

Table 1.1 Conceptual PlayWorld (Fleer, 2018, Copyright Conceptual PlayLab)

Pedagogical characteristics	Pedagogical practices that are planned
Selecting a story for the *Conceptual PlayWorld*	• Selecting a story that is enjoyable to children and adults. Summary of the story. • Building drama for the characters in the story. • Building empathy for the characters in the story. • A plot that lends itself to introducing a problem situation. Overview of the problem. • Being clear about the concept(s) and its relation to the story and play plot to be developed. • Adventures or journeys that spring from the plot (such as chapters).
Designing a *Conceptual PlayWorld* space	• Finding a space in the classroom/centre/outdoor area suitable for an imaginary *Conceptual PlayWorld* of the story. • Designing opportunities for child-initiated play in ways that develop the play plot further or explore concepts and make them more personally meaningful. • Planning different opportunities for children to represent their ideas and express their understandings.
Entering and exiting the *Conceptual PlayWorld* space	• Planning a routine for the whole group to enter and exit the *Conceptual PlayWorld* of the story where all the children are in the same imaginary situation. • Children choose characters as they enter the imaginary situation. • An adult is always a character in the story.
Planning the play inquiry or problem scenario	• The problem scenario is not scripted, but a general idea of the problem is planned. • The problem scenario is dramatic and engaging. • The problem invites children to investigate solutions to help the play in the *Conceptual PlayWorld*. • Being clear about the concepts that will be learned from solving the problem situation. Concepts are in service of the children's play.
Planning adult interactions to build conceptual learning in role	• Adults are not always the same character. Roles are not scripted. • Planning of who will have more knowledge and who will be present with the children to model solving the problem. There are different roles adults can take: Adults plan their role for the *Conceptual PlayWorld* to be **equally present** with the children, to **model practices** in their role, or to **need help** from the children. Their role can also **be together, with** the child leading (primordial we), where they literally cradle the child or hold their hand and together act out the role or solution.

Note. This table draws from Conceptual PlayWorld (Fleer, 2018, Copyright Conceptual PlayLab) and is used with permission.

group and are oriented to the story of *The Lonely Little Cactus*. Here, the problem will arise for the particular Conceptual PlayWorld for Wellbeing.

In each Conceptual PlayWorld for Wellbeing shown in this resource, we describe different ways to create spaces that provide opportunities for exploring concepts of wellbeing and social and emotional learning. The resource suggests different ideas and materials that can be used with minimal effort and preparation. We encourage educators and teachers to use our prompts to design novel and creative play spaces that further develop the story of *The Lonely Little Cactus* to explore the wellbeing concepts in a personally meaningful way.

Entering and exiting the Conceptual PlayWorld for Wellbeing space

This characteristic of a Conceptual PlayWorld for Wellbeing offers suggestions on how the whole group can enter and exit within the Conceptual PlayWorld for Wellbeing. All the children must be in the same imaginary situation. Here, children may choose characters (from the story) or choose to be themselves. We recommend that the educator or teacher is always a character in the story or at least acts as a human *prop* related to the story.

Planning the play inquiry or problem scenario

This characteristic of the Conceptual PlayWorld for Wellbeing presents a topic of inquiry or a problem scenario for the children to tackle.

The problem always arises in the imaginary situation.

To solve the problem, the children might go on adventures where they find things out. Or they might research something and then bring that knowledge into the play so that the play becomes more dramatic, exciting, and engaging.

The problem scenarios we present in this resource are designed to motivate children to find out more about their wellbeing. They are not scripted; instead, the general idea of the problem and journey is planned. For instance, planning may involve preparing a note to be read, crafting a treasure box to be found, or creating an invitation to a party to be received. The wellbeing concepts are also planned so that the research or journey the children take in the imaginary play is focused on growing their understanding of wellbeing.

In planning for the Conceptual PlayWorld for Wellbeing, the educator or teacher needs to articulate and make clear to the children what concepts will be learned for solving the problem. Each Conceptual PlayWorld for Wellbeing in this resource highlights the objective, and this objective explicit the wellbeing concept that is the focus of the problem and the imaginary play. The Conceptual PlayWorld for Wellbeing scenario problems are always explored so that the wellbeing concept services the children's play and helps their play to become deeper and richer.

Planning educator or teacher interactions to build wellbeing in a Conceptual PlayWorld

There are many roles the educator or teacher and the children can have in a Conceptual PlayWorld for Wellbeing, which creates a different learning dynamic to traditional early childhood education models.

Above and under positions

If someone is in the *above* position leading the ideas or play, someone will always be following in the *under* position. For example, one child in the above position may say to the educator or teacher in character as a bat, "I am Little Cactus. You be Bat." The adult in the under position responds by being Bat, perhaps asking Little Cactus in the above position, "What do I do?" The educator or teacher taking on the role of Wise Owl is an example of the *above* position.

Equal positions

The educator's or teacher's role within the Conceptual PlayWorld for Wellbeing can also be equally present with the children. In the *equal* position, two people (or even everyone in the group) can act equally and solve the problem together. There is no leader or follower. For example, Little Cactus and Bat can work together to solve the problem.

Primordial positions

The primordial is where a more competent player helps a child by holding their hand, cradling them when seated as though they are one, or doing the actions with them as though they are connected like twins. For example, we might see one child take the hand of another child and lead the child into the play scenario by saying, "We are both being Little Cactus today. We both feel lonely and want your help."

Final thoughts

Conceptual PlayWorlds for Wellbeing is an ideal way for children to explore wellbeing and social and emotional learning through play. We hope that readers of *The Lonely Little Cactus* will enjoy exploring the Conceptual PlayWorlds for Wellbeing in this resource to enhance children's wellbeing experiences.

Navigating your way around the Conceptual PlayWorlds for Wellbeing

We have provided a range of examples of Conceptual PlayWorld starters to support your implementation of a Conceptual PlayWorld for Wellbeing in your centre or classroom. As there are many examples provided, we have included a navigational tool in the form of a *roadmap* to help you quickly see what content is available for which wellbeing concept:

1. Identifying feelings
2. Coping (social support, problem-solving, or self-regulation)
3. Friendships (relationship building, working together, time with friends, social skills)
4. Positive emotions (happiness, joy, doing something you love, enjoyment, fun)
5. Relaxation strategies
6. Belonging and inclusion (working together, collaboration, joining in play, including others)

A roadmap to wellbeingv

Wellbeing concepts	Delivery mode	Conceptual PlayWorlds for Wellbeing
Identifying feelings	General classroom/centre materials and equipment	Chapter 5: Wise Mermaid's magic mirror
	Outside play equipment	Chapter 7: From being unhappy to feeling like a Superstar Snake
	General classroom/centre materials and equipment	Chapter 8: Anonymous acts of kindness
	Stop-motion animation	Chapter 9: Grand opening of *The Little Cactus* movie
Coping	General classroom/centre materials and equipment	Chapter 2: An urgent message from Eagle
	General classroom/centre materials and equipment. Optional outside space, like a sandpit.	Chapter 11: Message in a bottle
	Fairytale. Modified version of *Goldilocks and the Three Bears* & Google Earth for entering and exiting the Conceptual PlayWorld of the Deer Family's secret location in the forest.	Chapter 10: Feeling safe and designing a security system for the Deer Family
	General classroom/centre materials and equipment	Chapter 16: An acorn feast for Deer
	Outdoor area	Chapter 14: Relaxing in the snow
Friendship	General classroom/centre materials and equipment	Chapter 3: Little Cactus' quest in Friendship Land
	Different parts of the classroom/centre	Chapter 4: Little Cactus finds out how to organise a playdate
	Outdoors	Chapter 15: The Twinkle Party
	General classroom/centre materials and equipment	Chapter 13: Sneezing and wheezing: staying connected
	General classroom/centre materials and equipment	Chapter 20: A new friend
	General classroom/centre materials and equipment	Chapter 21: Compliments unlocked

Wellbeing concepts	Delivery mode	Conceptual PlayWorlds for Wellbeing
Positive emotions	Outside area	Chapter 17: Helping Eagle fly again
Relaxation strategies	Outdoor area	Chapter 14: Relaxing in the snow
	General classroom/centre materials and equipment	Chapter 18: Breathing buddies
Belonging and inclusion	General classroom/centre materials and equipment	Chapter 6: Helping Bat be included
	Multimedia presentation. Voice message left on phone from Snake.	Chapter 7: From being unhappy to feeling like a Superstar Snake
	General classroom/centre materials and equipment	Chapter 13: Sneezing and wheezing: staying connected
	General classroom/centre materials and equipment	Chapter 12: Working together for more than just treasure
	General classroom/centre materials and equipment	Chapter 19: Celebration of strengths
	General classroom/centre materials and equipment	Chapter 20: A new friend

Chapter two

AN URGENT MESSAGE FROM EAGLE

Introduction

Eagle is sitting on her perch high in the mountain and using her eagle eyes. She can see that Little Cactus is crying. Eagle is about to visit her friend and needs advice about how she can help.

Wellbeing theme: Coping

Learning Objective

1. Children explore the coping strategy of social support (that is, asking for help from a friend, educator, teacher, or parent).

Designing a Conceptual PlayWorld space for Wellbeing

You will need: a rope or piece of string, an old telephone or an object that can be used as a telephone, and a bell to simulate a phone ringing.

Entering and exiting the Conceptual PlayWorld space for Wellbeing

The Conceptual PlayWorld for Wellbeing is entered by stepping over a piece of string. The Conceptual PlayWorld is a blank, empty room. There are no paintings in the room. The room has no furniture. The only thing in the room is a phone in the middle of the room. It's on the floor.

DOI: 10.4324/9781003206569-2

Planning the play inquiry or problem scenario

Little Cactus experiences a range of feelings in the story, *The Lonely Little Cactus: A story about friendship and coping*, including feelings of anger, sadness, and loneliness. Young children need to learn to identify emotions and know that all feelings are important and normal. How we respond to emotions tends to matter the most. Coping is an important way to regulate our emotions, and this chapter explores the coping strategy of seeking social support and asking for help.

In this Conceptual PlayWorld for Wellbeing, children sit around the phone in a circle. The educator or teacher plays the role of Eagle. It is silent, and the children wait to see what happens – the phone rings.

The Eagle is on her perch (the educator or teacher may perch on a chair) and is using another telephone to ask for help from the children.

> *Children! I have a problem. I am on my perch high in the mountain. Because I have excellent eyesight, I can see my friend Little Cactus in the desert. He is crying. I did not even know cacti could cry!*
>
> *I think Little Cactus is crying because he feels lonely. I am planning on visiting him this afternoon. What advice can I give him? Children, can you help me?*

A discussion can follow about the importance of asking for help and how it can be a way to cope when things go wrong.

After the discussion, the children go on a "help adventure." They want to know who in their community helps others so they can find out:

- What helpers are there to care for others? Could some of them help Eagle look after Little Cactus? These are people like friends, teachers, educators, parents, or professionals in the community.

- How do they help others in different ways? Could some of their strategies be useful in helping Eagle help Little Cactus?

- How can they become a helper, and why would they want to help?

- What would they need to do to become a helper so they can support Eagle with the very sad Cactus?

The children set up a help desk using the phone they found in the empty room. Different children take on different roles as helpers. They make lanyards to name their special helper role.

More problems arise – other calls come in from different animals in the story who need help. Children practice being helped as well as being the helper.

Planning educator or teacher interactions to build wellbeing

In this Conceptual PlayWorld for Wellbeing, the educator or teacher takes on the role of Eagle, asking the children for advice and discussing different scenarios (under position). Eagle can suggest setting up a help centre with the children using their new skills to help all the different characters in the story (above position).

The characters in the under position can ask questions on the phone, such as: Have you ever asked someone for help? Who and why? How were you feeling at the time? Did asking for help fix things or change the way you were feeling?

Take away messages

Knowing how to ask for help is an important life skill. By exploring different problems, trying out helping strategies, and role-playing helping the animals who ring on the helpline, children are developing coping strategies of social support.

Adventures for going deeper

Explore another coping strategy that can help if a problem arises: the happiness list.

Little Cactus has been feeling rather upset lately and is having a difficult time. The educator or teacher – as Bat or Eagle – feels terrible that her friend is upset. In order to cheer up her friend, Bat decides to make a list of things that Little Cactus might enjoy doing or might like to find out if they can come up with some things that make them happy. However, Bat has difficulty coming up with a list that can be helpful. Can the children help?

With a colourful marker and a whiteboard or large piece of paper, start making "Little Cactus' Happiness List." What do the children think Little Cactus might like? Are there specific activities Little Cactus might like? Certain snacks or treats? If the children struggle, prompt them with Little Cactus' enjoyment of singing from the book.

After the children have compiled a decently long list, ask them how they came up with the list. What types of things did they think about while doing so? Did they think about the kind of things animals like? What about thinking about what they like?

Ask the children to make their own "Happiness List" full of small things they enjoy that make them feel good. Ask children to make their lists creatively and encourage them to draw pictures or use their favourite colours. Remind children that they can keep these lists for times they are feeling sad, discouraged, or upset, and that putting easy but fun things on the list will make the list even more helpful.

Chapter three

LITTLE CACTUS' QUEST IN FRIENDSHIP LAND

Introduction

When Little Cactus tries to visit Friendship Land and learn about friendship from Wise Owl, he discovers that he is stuck on the path! He can't move! Can the children help him on his journey?

Wellbeing theme: Friendship

Learning Objectives

1. Children explore friendship and how it is developed and maintained.

Designing a Conceptual PlayWorld for Wellbeing space

You will need a tree in the yard of the preschool or centre to form the basis of Friendship Land. The tree is where Wise Owl lives. A soft toy owl can be placed in the tree. Tape small Owl Boxes along the path, with questions about friendship inside. Bring along a bag of snacks for Owl to share.

Entering and exiting the Conceptual PlayWorld for Wellbeing space

The children can enter and exit Friendship Land through a large Owl Box (climbing frame covered with a cloth sheet). The entrance has a sign hanging on it: "Welcome to Friendship Land."

DOI: 10.4324/9781003206569-3

Planning the play inquiry or problem scenario

Little Cactus finds he cannot move at all – his feet are stuck on the path. He receives a message from Wise Owl by emergency pigeon post.

Dear Little Cactus,

Oh no! I can see that you are stuck on the path. Unfortunately, our emergency security system has been activated by accident. You will need to answer some questions about Friendship to be able to visit me. You will see the questions in the boxes. Every time you answer one, you will unstick and move to the next one.

Little Cactus is very distressed. He came to Friendship Land to find some answers like: What is a friend? How do you make friends? How do you keep friends? And now there are even more! That's OK. The children – in their animal characters – can help him.

Some Questions

- How do you know when someone is your friend?

- What are some things friends do that make you feel happy?

- What are some things children can do to help them make and keep friends?

- What should children do if they upset a friend?

- How do you know if someone is feeling left out?

- How can children include someone who might not feel they have someone to play with?

When Little Cactus and his animal friends answer each of the questions, they hear an owl hoot. Terrific answer! Bing! You can go to the next Owl Box.

The game progresses and, finally, they come to the last Owl Box. There is a message inside:

Congratulations, Little Cactus and children. You have given such thoughtful answers. The way should now be free to come to my tree.

Would you like to have a snack picnic with me?

The children arrive at the tree and share a picnic with Wise Owl, who can reflect on some of the answers and the ways that the children have already shown friendship towards Little Cactus.

They exit the Conceptual PlayWorld. Sometime later, the children can receive a package from Wise Owl – he has sent them a special book with their answers to keep in their classroom.

Planning educator or teacher interactions to build wellbeing

In the Conceptual PlayWorld for Wellbeing, the educator or teacher takes on the role of Little Cactus and summarises the children's advice. A second educator or teacher can take on the role of Wise Owl.

The educator or teacher can also surreptitiously record the answers from the children to prepare the Friendship Book that Wise Owl will send after they exit the Conceptual PlayWorld.

Take away messages

Friendships matter for children. Knowing how to be a friend is essential for children's wellbeing. It is more than being friendly. It is about developing relationship skills that they will use throughout their lives.

Adventures for going deeper

In this Conceptual PlayWorld for Wellbeing, you and your children went on an adventure to learn about friendship skills. To bring more thinking about the concept and imagination to the journey, you and the children could go on a second adventure with some new problems that regularly arise in young children's friendships: managing conflict and making decisions.

One evening, all the animals and Little Cactus are beginning a playdate but cannot agree on what to do together. Deer and Little Cactus would like to go on a hike. Porcupine and Bat would much rather stay and wait for nighttime to stargaze. They have also invited their new friend, Snake, and want to make sure their new friend has lots of fun with them for their first-ever playdate. The group wants to do different things, but they all agree that the most important thing is that they can spend time together and be friends during the playdate. Still, they just do not know what to do!

Ask the children what advice they would give the friends and what they think the group should do for the day. How could they compromise so that everyone is happy? How will they decide what to do? How will they make sure everyone is having fun?

Chapter four

LITTLE CACTUS FINDS OUT HOW TO ORGANISE A PLAYDATE

Introduction

In the story, Little Cactus cannot find a friend and feels lonely. He wants to be able to play with other children and, most of all, have a playdate, but he does not know how to set one up. Can the children help?

Wellbeing theme: Friendships

Learning Objectives

1. Children will have an opportunity to design a playdate.
2. Children will be able to add to a play narrative.

 Designing a Conceptual PlayWorld for Wellbeing space

The home corner or an area of the classroom is turned into the Cactus House. A table and some chairs are arranged as though it was a dining table and kitchen area. Soft cushions are on the floor, as though it were the family room for relaxing and playing.

The desert can be an outdoor play space.

DOI: 10.4324/9781003206569-4

Entering and exiting the Conceptual PlayWorld for Wellbeing space

This scenario has two play spaces: the desert and the Cactus House. A door can signify entering the desert, where the children can enter and exit. An outdoor space would work well for this.

A large cardboard box in the desert with a cut-out door represents the entrance to the Cactus House. The children go through the door to enter and exit the Cactus House.

Planning the play inquiry or problem scenario

In the story, Little Cactus cannot find a friend and feels lonely. On this occasion, Little Cactus wants to learn how to play with others.

The children and educators or teachers, in character as various animals from the book, go on a desert adventure to visit Little Cactus. However, when they get there, they cannot find him anywhere.

Maybe he is at Cactus House?

The children go to visit Little Cactus at home. When they get there, he does not want to go outside. He calls out from the inside: "I don't know how to play with other people, can you help?"

The educator or teacher plays the role of Little Cactus in this scenario. The children, in character as the different animals, can offer suggestions on different strategies Little Cactus can try.

Little Cactus says through the door: "How will I remember all of these ideas? I'm so shy! Can you draw me pictures or write them down for me?"

The children can then exit the Conceptual PlayWorld. They can search for ideas or websites about friendships, or you can read children's books about friendships. They can prepare a mind map of ideas. Children can draw pictures of children playing together and include ideas they want to share with Little Cactus.

One of the ideas should be to organise a playdate. If the children don't suggest one, the educator or teacher can prompt this.

They can then re-enter the desert and visit Cactus House. This time, Little Cactus is brave enough to come outside and sit with the children.

Each child, in character, can share their ideas with Little Cactus and give him their drawings to pin up. Make sure the playdate idea comes last.

When Little Cactus hears about the playdate, he can say, "That is what I want more than anything in the world! But how do I go about organising one?"

The children, in character, along with the educator or teacher as Little Cactus, sit in a circle outside Cactus House and talk through ideas like creating an invitation with a kind message, planning the playdate, and creating a welcoming space. What if Little Cactus is feeling shy?

The educator or teacher can reflect on aspects of the story with Little Cactus. For example, Little Cactus loves to sing. Little Cactus could think about his friend. Does he also like to sing? Maybe they can play a karaoke game. Which ideas do the children like the best? Which ones work for them? Little Cactus summarises these at the end and says thank you!

The children can then exit the Conceptual PlayWorld. A little while later, they receive a letter from Little Cactus to say that he got enough courage to ask his friend Deer for a playdate and they had so much fun dressing up and singing karaoke (you could even include a picture of the educator or teacher as Little Cactus and another educator or teacher as Deer singing into a microphone).

Little Cactus said he had created a wall of friendship at Cactus House. You can come along and visit anytime you like!

(The wall of friendship could become an installation in the learning space for the children to reflect on.)

Planning educator or teacher interactions to build wellbeing

The educator or teacher in the Conceptual PlayWorld can play Little Cactus – the under position. A second educator or teacher, if there is one, can take on one of the story's characters.

Take away messages

Children sometimes need help joining in established play. This Conceptual PlayWorld for Wellbeing helps children develop skills in entering play, being a play partner, and joining the existing play narrative. The playdate and party plan can help children think about how to do these things by preparing a plan, allowing them to test out their ideas, and creating an experience for them to reflect on.

Adventures for going deeper

In this Conceptual PlayWorld for Wellbeing, you and your children went on an adventure to learn how to play with others. To bring more thinking about the concept and imagination to the journey, you and the children could go on a second adventure with a new problem, as follows:

During a playdate with Bat and Porcupine, Little Cactus suggests playing his favourite game, Tic-Tac-Toe. When setting up the game, Little Cactus hands a marker to Bat and keeps one for himself, telling Porcupine that they can't play right now because the game is only for two players.

Divide the children, as able, into groups of three, with each child taking the role of one of the friends (Little Cactus, Porcupine, and Bat). In some cases, it may be important to have an educator or teacher or other adult take the role of Porcupine so that children do not risk feeling left out. Ask the children to reflect on how each friend in the group may feel, gently guiding them to how Porcupine may feel about being unable to play with her friends.

Prompt the children to problem-solve the best way to include Porcupine in their game or play (this may include taking turns with the game, forming teams, or even playing a different game entirely). The important part is that the children can compromise and problem-solve a solution that would make everyone feel included.

Chapter five

WISE MERMAID'S MAGIC MIRROR

Introduction

Little Cactus is in a pickle. He received an invitation from Wise Mermaid to visit her in Magical Water World, but he has not been able to gain entry to the world because he does not understand enough about feelings. Can his friends help him?

Wellbeing theme: Identifying feelings

Learning Objectives

1. Children will have the opportunity to recognise and name emotions.
2. Children will practice reading others' emotional expressions and responding appropriately.

 Designing a Conceptual PlayWorld for Wellbeing space

You will need a large blue painter's drop sheet to create a Magical Water World. Scattered all over the blue imaginary water are seashells, plastic strips acting as seaweed, soft toys, and sprinkled sand.

Print out two sets of cards with different facial expressions on them. Scatter one set in the sand.

Create a "magic mermaid mirror" (a screen that can play all the different expressions from the children or shell to put on an iPad or phone) and prepare a special sound that will show that Magical Water World is now open.

DOI: 10.4324/9781003206569-5

Entering and exiting the Conceptual PlayWorld for Wellbeing space

Paper footprints are stuck on the floor leading to Magical Water World. At the entrance is a sign "You are now entering Magical Water World. Before entering, select a card (images of different facial expressions)."

Planning the play inquiry or problem scenario

In the Conceptual PlayWorld for Wellbeing, the children receive a message from Little Cactus asking for their help. He says to follow the footprints to find him in Magical Water World.

When they arrive, they see Wise Mermaid sitting next to Little Cactus (this can be a teacher or another educator or teacher), who looks very sad. What is wrong with Little Cactus?

Wise Mermaid explains that a spell to enter the Magical Water World needs to be unlocked – and the way to unlock it is to name all the different feelings on the cards. Little Cactus has been having trouble. Can the children help?

Wise Mermaid offers the children a feelings card, and they each wait to talk to Wise Mermaid. "Who is entering my world?" The children respond in character. Then she asks: "And what does your card show?"

The children name the feeling and then act it out. Wise Mermaid films them on an Ipad, tablet or phone. She then invites them to find a matching card in the sand and come and sit next to Little Cactus.

After everybody is finished, there is a magical bell sound and the entrance to Magical Water World is opened. Everybody can now enter and play inside.

After a time, play the sound again, and Wise Mermaid asks if Little Cactus is feeling more confident about feelings. He replies yes – but would like to see all the faces of the children again.

Wise Mermaid can then play the videos and look at the recordings of their emotions. The children talk about what they see and share what they notice with Little Cactus.

When they are done, Little Cactus says thank you – he will take all this information home to the desert. The magical bell chimes again, and the children then exit the Conceptual PlayWorld.

Planning educator or teacher interactions to build wellbeing

The educator or teacher can take the Wise Mermaid role and interpret Little Cactus' feelings. The children take the lead and can teach Little Cactus about the emotions on their cards.

Take away messages

Recognition of emotional expressions is vital for reading how others feel and is the first step in recognising and naming one's own feelings. Both skills are learned and lead to emotional regulation over time. However, first children need a lot of practice recognising emotions to support their growing emotional regulation.

Adventures for going deeper

In this Conceptual PlayWorld for Wellbeing, you and your children went on an adventure to explore emotions. Try the following exercise for further reflection.

Invite the children to name emotions and use prompts, if necessary. Some ideas can be anxious, scared, angry, or excited. Prompt children to think of situations where they, or the characters in the story, may have felt this way.

Explain that when you have strong emotions, you can feel them in your body, just like a touch or a tickle. Provide examples of your own experiences. For example: When I get scared, my brain feels like it is an untuned radio and I cannot think straight. Or: When I am sad, I feel like there is a big rain cloud on my head.

Give your students a blank outline of a person and ask them to draw how a specific emotion feels in their body. After the drawings are complete, ask the students to share their ideas with the group.

You can also prompt discussions about how different students experience the same emotions. You can also prompt the students to think of ways that the animal characters feel emotions in their bodies. For example: When Porcupine is scared, his quills tense up, but when Deer is scared, she can just freeze.

Chapter six

HELPING BAT BE INCLUDED

Introduction

Bat has an invitation to go to a dance party at Little Cactus' house, but she is worried because her hearing is not working very well after an accident with a tree. Bat thinks she will not be able to take part and, most of all, will not be included in the fun – can the children help her?

Wellbeing theme: Belonging and inclusion

Learning Objectives

1. Children can learn that not feeling included can make others feel left out.
2. Children have an opportunity to recognise when someone is left out.
3. Children will learn ways to help others feel included.

Designing a Conceptual PlayWorld for Wellbeing space

The desert is recreated in the sandpit of the outdoor area. Potted plants of succulents (or big drawings of them) are placed around the area as indicative of desert plant life.

Entering and exiting the Conceptual PlayWorld for Wellbeing space

A set of chimes made from a metal coat hanger with lengths of string and objects dangling freely are placed on an outdoor trestle or other structure (such as a tree).

The children enter and exit Little Cactus' desert by banging on the chimes with a metal stick or wooden spoon for a short musical performance.

DOI: 10.4324/9781003206569-6

Planning the play inquiry or problem scenario

The children enter the Conceptual PlayWorld in character and find a message from Bat stuck on a cactus:

> *Dear Children,*
>
> *I have an invitation to go to a dance party from Little Cactus. I am very worried because I had an accident with a tree and my sonar hearing has been affected.*
>
> *It's a big problem because sound is how I find my way, and even if I can find Little Cactus' dance party, I won't hear the music and can't dance. I will feel left out. Can you help me?*
>
> *Your friend,*
>
> *Bat*

The children try to find out as many things as they can about bats to work out how to help. They might investigate questions such as:

- How do bats communicate?

- How do bats fly at night?

- Can they hear music?

- How do they feel the vibrations?

- What do they like to eat?

The children decide to help by working out the best way to support Bat in feeling included. So, they try out a few strategies. Examples could be:

1. Design musical instruments that create different vibrations (short and high, long and low).
2. Make funnels out of paper to amplify the sounds of their instruments.
3. Preparing different musical pieces with performances to see if that will help.

The children test out their ideas with Bat and decide to go to the party with her to try out their suggestions together. Bat, Little Cactus, and all the animals have a great time dancing and singing their favourite songs.

Bat thanks the children for their help. They start to exit the Conceptual PlayWorld when they receive a video message. It is from Bat! The party ends.

Children, guess what! My hearing has returned. Thank goodness. Everything has gone back to normal. Thank you so much for supporting me at the dance party. All your suggestions were excellent.

But do you know what was the best? You tried to find out about my needs and got me involved in deciding what helped me feel included. I am going to remember your kindness for a long time to come.

Spend some time talking together about Bat's message before exiting the Conceptual PlayWorld.

Planning educator or teacher interactions to build wellbeing

The educator or teacher takes on the under position in this Conceptual PlayWorld, using a puppet to represent Bat.

The children adopt the above position as they research bats, prepare the dance party materials, and present their ideas.

When the children talk about how important it was for Bat to say what mattered to her, they adopt an equal position.

Take away messages

All children like to feel included. However, they do not always know how to help others be included. Through the children researching what Bat needs and then consulting with Bat about the options they have come up with, they are developing strategies for helping others feel and be included.

Adventures for going deeper

In this Conceptual PlayWorld for Wellbeing, you and your children went on an adventure to help Bat feel included even though she lost her sonar. You can also take the opportunity to research what it means to be a friend.

Ask your students to think about what it means to be a friend and what specific things friends do for each other.

On a whiteboard or large piece of paper, create two columns: what makes a good friend and what makes a not-so-good friend. Take suggestions from students and ask which column their answers belong in.

If there is uncertainty, ask the group for feedback and facilitate a discussion. It might not always be clear, so help students discuss context and situations for different behaviours.

After the list is complete, ask them to reflect on the traits and behaviours they exhibit as friends. Which of the "good friend" behaviours can they do more often?

Chapter seven

FROM BEING UNHAPPY TO FEELING LIKE A SUPERSTAR SNAKE

Introduction

Snake has lived in the desert forever, but every time she tries to welcome newcomers, they scream and run away. She has lost all confidence and feels unloved and alone. Can the children help her?

Wellbeing theme: Belonging and Inclusion and Coping

Learning Objectives

1. Children will practice recognising fear as an emotion.
2. Children will be able to understand that fear can cause a flight response.
3. Children will be able to identify that fear can make a person respond negatively in a situation.

 Designing a Conceptual PlayWorld for Wellbeing space

An outdoor tunnel acts as a snake hole. It is placed in the sandpit or outdoor play area near other structures to act as cover. If you do not have a tunnel, a large sheet sewn along one side can be fitted to a cardboard box with a cut-out opening that is wide enough for children to crawl through the box and sheet.

DOI: 10.4324/9781003206569-7

Entering and exiting the Conceptual PlayWorld for Wellbeing space

A sign on the front of the tunnel reads "Caution Beware of Snakes" On the back, have a sign that says "Friendly Snake Ahead."

 ## *Planning the play inquiry or problem scenario*

When the children enter the tunnel and crawl out to the other side, Snake appears to welcome them into her home. As might be expected, upon first meeting with Snake the children scream with fear. The children leave through the tunnel and find Cactus (educator or teacher in character) waiting for them. The children tell Cactus about their adventure of meeting Snake.

As the children share their experiences and discuss if or how they fear snakes, Cactus receives a phone call from Snake who is crying (this can be a pre-recorded message done by the educator or teacher). Cactus puts the phone on speaker so all the children can hear the message.

> *Hello Cactus, I have been living in the desert for a long time. Every time someone comes to visit me, they scream and run away. Sob sob sob . . . I am feeling so unloved, not understood, and miserable. What can I do? Sob sob sob . . . How can others better understand me? I have to go now, goodbye. Sob sob sob*

The educator or teacher talks to the children about how Snake is feeling and records a mind map of the different feelings Snake expresses. They then prepare a second mind map of what the children know about snakes and how they came to learn that information.

Some Ideas Little Cactus can Suggest

- What kind of snake is Snake? (Snake is not dangerous)
- Are all snakes dangerous?
- How are snakes good for the ecosystem?
- How do you look after snakes?
- How do you stay safe around snakes?

Snake can be reached by text or voice message to answer questions.

Now that the children know that Snake is not dangerous, Cactus suggests that they find a way to help Snake be accepted by visitors when they crawl through the snake hole and arrive in her home.

The children can then think of ideas that show visitors that Snake is safe, happy, and to help them understand more about all snakes. They flip the sign and crawl through the snake hole to share their ideas with Snake and ask her if they can take photos of her or create videos of her doing all sorts of happy and kind snake activities.

The children can then create a presentation that their educators, teachers, or children from another class can experience when they go down the snake hole. This presentation can even include a multimedia presentation that presents ideas in different ways and forms.

On a subsequent visit, before entering the snake hole, Cactus puts his phone on speaker so all the children can hear a message from Snake that was left while they were all working:

> *Dear Children . . . It is Snake calling. I have now had many visitors to my snake home, and no one has run away. They all say how happy they are to meet me. Apparently, I am a superstar. They come to ask for my autograph. I feel so loved and wanted now. They take photos of me – lots of selfies. They understand me now. No one is frightened of me anymore. Thank you so much for helping me. Your solution to the problem has worked. Bye from Superstar Snake.*

 ### *Planning educator or teacher interactions to build wellbeing*

The children can go in character down the snake hole. One child can be a Snake. The educator or teacher takes on the above position as Little Cactus when she plays the Snake's message and can call Snake to ask questions.

As the children research and find solutions, they are taking on the equal position in the play.

Take away messages

Fear is an emotional response (strong emotion with flight action) connected with how others show their fear response in social situations. Children may believe that a fear of something is based on facts, and do not think that it could also be a stereotype that they have learned to mimic (associated fear response with something specific, like a snake or spider).

Researching something you may be frightened of brings understanding, and this can lead to new thinking and ways of responding to the same situation, such as when seeing a snake or spider.

Adventures for going deeper

In this Conceptual PlayWorld for Wellbeing, you and your children went on an adventure into the desert through a snake hole. Try going on a second adventure into the desert with a new problem to bring more thinking about the concept and imagination to the journey.

Sometimes a thunderstorm might happen in the desert. Imagine a storm suddenly rolling in above the animal friends during a playdate with Snake. During their playdate, the other animals notice that Porcupine is afraid of the lightning and loud thunder. Consider playing ambient rain or thunderstorm noises to add to the feeling in the room.

The educator or teacher adopts the role of Porcupine and because she is scared, all her quills are raised. The children adopt the roles of the animals – or can be Porcupine's new human friends – and help her during the storm.

Ask the children to think of coping skills that can be used for Porcupine. What do they do when they are scared that makes them feel safer or calmer? Children should demonstrate these skills and walk through the skills with Porcupine, with all students practicing the skills as they go.

Consider making a list of these skills to be posted or reviewed later if children need to use them. Ask the children to think of times they have been afraid or upset by something. Can they name any of these instances? How did they feel after using their own coping skills?

As Porcupine's fears diminish, the quills go down and she can start to feel calmer.

Chapter eight

KINDNESS CHAMPIONS

Introduction

The animal friends decide to visit Little Cactus but need to go over High Desert Pass. It's very hot and difficult, but it is made easier by treasures from the Kindness Fairies. However, at the top of the pass, they find an alarming message – the Kindness Fairies have lost their powers. Can the children help them?

Wellbeing theme: Friendships

Learning Objectives

1. Children will have opportunities to express kindness – identifying what kindness means.
2. Children will find different ways to respond to acts of kindness.
3. Children will identify how it feels to receive kindness from others.

 Designing a Conceptual PlayWorld for Wellbeing space

The outdoor area is imagined as a desert. Educators or teachers may use a yellow fabric to represent sand, the outside sand pit, or a space labelled with a sign.

Prepare notes and treasures as outlined in the play inquiry, as well as a sheet children can take home as part of a "Kindness Investigation".

 Entering and exiting the Conceptual PlayWorld for Wellbeing space

A sign to the entrance of the desert reads: *This way to High Desert Pass.* The children squeeze between two structures (such as concrete cylinders or large electrical cable rolls) that simulate a rocky canyon entrance to the desert.

DOI: 10.4324/9781003206569-8

Planning the play inquiry or problem scenario

After reading the story of Little Cactus, the children – as their animal characters – decide to visit the Cactus to see how he is doing. They have not visited for a while. However, a big rockfall has blocked the road to his house and they need to go over High Desert Pass.

They check the weather by looking at the Bureau of Meteorology (BOM) website (simulated) and find it has been unusually hot. It is going to be a big challenge.

As they climb, it is even hotter than expected. They find a tree to rest under halfway there until it gets cooler. Everybody falls asleep.

When they wake up, they find that all their water has gone and they are thirsty. They find a note next to their empty water bottles. "There is a well just ahead. You can get more water there."

When they get to the well, there is a box on it. Inside, they find a bucket and a message:

> *Please feel free to use our well if you are thirsty. You might want to keep the bucket for other treasures you find on the way up to High Desert Pass. We hope it helps!*
>   *Love, the Kindness Fairies of the Desert*

After they are refreshed from the water, the children continue their climb. It's still very hot and difficult, but they start to find other treasure boxes. There are ten in total. Inside each box is a message and sometimes a small gift. For example:

Message 1

Here are some big Fairy hugs for you (lots of printed-out hug emojis, for example). You are doing great!

Message 2

We heard that it is hot in the desert. Here are some fans to keep you cool.

The children gather the gifts and messages and read them. They reach the top and find Little Cactus waiting there for a picnic. He is amazed at the gifts and how strong the children are.

They sit in a circle, eat the picnic, and talk about the gifts. Did finding the gifts and receiving the kindness help them feel better? Did they feel like they could manage the challenge of getting over High Desert Pass?

Just as they finish up, Little Cactus spies one last treasure box. It is an urgent message from the Kindness Fairies, asking for help.

Dear children,

Can you please help us! After we wrote our last message, a terrible troll came along and stole all our ideas about kindness. Now we cannot think of anything at all and we are very sad. Can you please talk to your families about what they think kindness is and some ways to show kindness? Once we get your messages, it will restore our powers and we will be able to help lots more people.

Love, the Kindness Fairies of the Desert

The children return to the classroom and decide to go on a kindness investigation. They can take home a special sheet they can fill in with their families. Then, when they return to the class, they can discuss the ideas as a group. Then, each child can put their kindness ideas in a treasure box.

The children can return to High Desert Pass – in character – by hot air balloon this time and leave the treasure boxes for the Kindness Fairies. You might like to use boxes, sheets, or old baskets to create the balloon.

They return to the classroom in a hot air balloon. Before they exit the Conceptual PlayWorld, they find a note pinned to the exit. It reads:

Dear Children,

We received all your messages and ideas about kindness. You were very kind to make all that effort to talk to your families and to share them. As soon as we started reading your messages, we could feel our kindness powers coming back! Thank you so much, children! You are our Champions of Kindness.

Planning educator or teacher interactions to build wellbeing

The educator or teacher takes on the role of a character in the book and travels with the children up to the High Desert Pass. At the top, the educator or teacher can take on the role of Little Cactus to talk about kindness and acts of kindness. Together in the classroom, you prepare the kindness ideas and treasure boxes to help the Kindness Fairies.

Take away messages

Being kind and showing kindness can feel rewarding for the person who gives it. However, it is also a wonderful feeling to know someone cares about you and shows this by doing something kind. Acts of kindness and being kind can look and feel differently to the receiver and to the giver. How it feels to give and receive kindness is what matters. Are acts of kindness a real treasure?

Adventures for going deeper

In this Conceptual PlayWorld for Wellbeing, you and your children went on an adventure to visit Little Cactus and help the Kindness Fairies of the Desert. To bring more thinking about the concept and imagination to the journey, you and the children could set up a net to catch positivity and kindness in your classroom for a week (or even longer). As children observe these moments, have them write them down, draw a picture, or tell an educator or teacher. It can then be added to the net. As the net gets full, it's a visual cue of the positive moments and supports the children to be more attentive to the good things happening around them.

Chapter nine

GRAND OPENING OF THE LITTLE CACTUS MOVIE

Introduction

Camera! Lights! Action! There is a film in the making, and everyone is learning about feelings because, after all, how can you be a good actor if you cannot convey feelings?

Wellbeing theme: Identifying feelings

Learning Objectives

1. Children will be able to identify the emotional expressions of others.
2. Children will have an opportunity to understand that emotions can be differentially expressed by children, families, and cultural communities.

 ## *Designing a Conceptual PlayWorld for Wellbeing space*

The preschool/classroom is transformed into a movie production studio.

 ## *Entering and exiting the Conceptual PlayWorld for Wellbeing space*

To enter and exit the studio, children show their security pass – as an actor, camera operator, musical producer, costume designer, emotions researcher (or psychologist), soft toy engineer, storyboard artist, and set designer, et cetera.

 ## *Planning the play inquiry or problem scenario*

After reading the story, the educator or teacher turns to the final page and finds a note from the local TV station inviting them to make a movie about the story.

DOI: 10.4324/9781003206569-9

The children use soft toys of all the characters for their stop-motion animation, but they have a problem. The soft toys do not show emotions and they need to feature them in their stop-motion animation. How can they solve this problem?

The children investigate emotions, finding out how different people in their community show emotions. What kinds of emotions are expressed, and what do they look like? The children ask their interviewees to show them different emotions. They take photos and video clips of the expressions, such as those shown by Grandma, their baby sister, the neighbour, the educators or teachers in the school, and so on. Children can also draw expressions as an alternative to photos.

With this visual information, they draw pictures of expressions onto circular cards and put these on Little Cactus' face and the relevant characters in the story. The children prepare a storyboard of the Little Cactus movie and put the cards on the relevant representation of the screen in their storyboard. Then they role-play the whole story themselves, checking that each expression is suitable for the moment in the story. The children tell the story and make their movie of the story of Little Cactus.

The children plan and prepare for the grand opening of their movie, make popcorn, give out tickets, seat the audience, and then screen their movie.

 ## *Planning educator or teacher interactions to build wellbeing*

The educator or teacher adopts the above position to show the children a behind-the-scenes tour of a studio. Guide them as you would on an excursion or use YouTube or other immersive experiences such as flash cards with photos of the studio or by using a book. You can devise a clapperboard, introduce studios-specific language like "action," "rolling," "cut," and "that's a wrap," as well as some props, like a director's chair or a megaphone.

The children and educator or teacher work together to plan how they will make their movie – the equal position in the play. The children select which security pass and role they will take in the movie. As they research emotions, they adopt the under position; and, if they direct others, they adopt the above position.

Take away messages

Assigning emotions to soft toys could be a difficult exercise because the children have to be able to recognise an emotional expression, name it, and then demonstrate it themselves. Then they need to represent it as symbols (drawing) and then assign it to a soft toy. This experience supports them to realise emotional expressions represent a particular feeling, and that some people show their emotional expressions differently.

Adventures for going deeper

In this Conceptual PlayWorld for Wellbeing, you and your children made a movie about Little Cactus that was screened at a grand opening. To bring more thinking about the concept and imagination to the journey, do more research about emotions.

Ask students to think about how characters from the story or Little Cactus might show various emotions. Either prompt students to think about how they would show specific emotions or begin the activity by asking students to work together to make a list of emotions. These emotions might include feeling nervous, happy, jealous, anger, annoyed, surprised, or excited.

Ask students to identify ways in which other people might express these emotions. What faces might people make? What would their body language look like? What might they say? Close the discussion with a conversation about why it is important to understand how others are feeling.

Chapter ten

FEELING SAFE AND DESIGNING A SECURITY SYSTEM FOR THE DEER FAMILY

Introduction

Like Goldilocks, the Lonely Little Cactus decides to explore the forest, finds a beautiful hidden glen, and plays there. He does not know it is a special, secret spot for the Deer family. When the Deer family returns, they are very worried about unknown intruders. Can the children help them feel safe?

Wellbeing theme: Coping

Learning Objectives

1. Children will understand the importance of feeling safe for their wellbeing.
2. Children will be able to understand the different ways of being safe.

 ## Designing a Conceptual PlayWorld for Wellbeing space

The garden of an outdoor area can be used as the Deer's forest. It is a secret location, and no one knows where the Deer family lives.

 ## *Entering and exiting the Conceptual PlayWorld for Wellbeing space*

There is a pathway leading to the forest. Google Maps (or an alternative map option, online or offline) plots the path into the forest and out again.

DOI: 10.4324/9781003206569-10

Planning the play inquiry or problem scenario

Little Cactus goes walking in the forest and finds a secret location. It feels really special. He wishes he had a friend to play there with him.

He finds sweet grass and rolls in each patch: a small one, a middle-sized one, and a large one. Then he sees a tree stump playground and jumps on each one – small, medium, and tall. He leaves some prickles behind.

Finally, Little Cactus is tired and sees three different-sized dry grass nests. He snuggles into each and eventually finds the smallest one fits him well. He has a nap, and when he wakes up, it is nearly nighttime. Shocked and panicked, Little Cactus jumps out of the dry grass nest, accidentally destroying it, and runs home.

When the sun rises the next day, the Deer family visits their special place. They notice the flattened grass – who has been playing with our food? Mama Deer notices the tree stumps are full of prickles – who has left these terrible spikes? Then, finally, they notice the destroyed nest and roar loudly with worry. There are intruders in our glen! Are the wolves returning to eat them?

The Deer family feels unsafe and decides they need to set up a security system. They enlist the help of Wise Eagle and think about all the different elements that they can use. As it's in a forest, you may even use Google Earth to map out different paths that need to be considered.

They set up the system and head home. The next day, Little Cactus returns to the glen. He just loved it there. As he arrives, all the alarms go off, and he is so scared. He tries to run away, but trips on a stick, hurting his ankle.

The Deer family arrives, ready to fight the wolves. Then they notice Little Cactus, sitting on the forest floor and crying. Poor Cactus is so scared, and his ankle hurts.

The Deer parents run home to get some ice and bandages. Little Deer stays and holds his hand. As the Deer parents return, Wise Eagle arrives and figures out what has happened – it is all a big misunderstanding.

The educator or teacher, as Wise Eagle, leads a discussion about what it means to feel safe for each of the characters. Wise Eagle asks the children if they have any solutions. Wise Eagle can prompt the characters with ideas. For example:

- The Deer family says Little Cactus is welcome to visit their place anytime.

- The Deer family helps Little Cactus build his own nest, a patch of sweet grass, and a fourth stump.

- The Deer family asks Little Cactus if he could phone first before visiting so the alarm does not go off.

- Little Cactus is so happy to feel included, he bravely asks the Deer family if he could join their next family picnic.

- Can children – as their animal characters – create signs that will help other animals feel safe in the forest?

Finally, with his ankle feeling better, the Deer family offers to give Little Cactus a ride home on their backs, and they exit the Conceptual PlayWorld.

 Planning educator or teacher interactions to build wellbeing

The educator or teacher adopts the character of Wise Eagle in the above position to support the Deer family and Little Cactus finding different solutions. The children adopt the positions of Little Cactus and the Deer family.

Take away messages

Feelings of safety are essential for a child's wellbeing, as they form one of our most basic and critical psychological needs for healthy human development. When a child's safety is threatened, those children who are equipped with skills to cope with adversities and challenges, such as problem-solving skills, are more likely to be resilient.

Adventures for going deeper

In this Conceptual PlayWorld for Wellbeing, you and your children went on an adventure and prepared a security system for the Deer family to keep them safe. To bring more thinking about the concept and imagination, explore what it means to feel safe.

Ask students to sit quietly, potentially with their eyes closed, and think of a place they have felt safe before or imagine where they would feel safe. This place may be real or imaginary, and may include any features, depending on the child's preference.

The goal is to let the child think of an entirely positive, safe, and calming place that is perfect for them. Encourage students to think creatively and for as long as they may need to. Once they have an idea, ask students if they would like to share their safe place and what it means to be safe.

If time allows, provide students with paper and writing utensils, such as markers or coloured pencils, and allow them to draw a representation of their safe place while playing calming music or sounds. Tell students that they can keep this drawing with them for times when they feel angry, overwhelmed, afraid, threatened, or otherwise upset and can imagine going into their safe place in their mind, just as they practiced before making their drawing.

Have students practice thinking of their safe place again and tell them that their safe place can change over time, but the important thing is that they can draw the place in their mind and imagine it when they need to.

Chapter eleven

MESSAGE IN A BOTTLE

Introduction

Porcupine finds a bottle in the sand, and it has a message in it from Little Cactus, who is stranded on a desert island and is feeling lonely. However, they are separated by the ocean. How can Porcupine and his friends help when they are so far away?

Wellbeing Theme: Coping

Learning Objectives

1. Children will experience a problem-solving scenario.
2. Children will be able to identify a variety of coping strategies.
3. Children will be able to identify that coping strategies can vary depending on the situation and who is using them.

Designing a Conceptual PlayWorld for Wellbeing space

Source a piece of fabric representing sand or an ocean in a beach scene. A hula-hoop or circle made with string can be used to represent a magic portal. Alternatively, an existing outside space could work, such as the sandpit.

Entering and exiting the Conceptual PlayWorld for Wellbeing space

The educator or teacher, as Porcupine, leads children to enter the Conceptual PlayWorld for Wellbeing through a magic portal and they find themselves in the sandy dunes.

DOI: 10.4324/9781003206569-11

Planning the play inquiry or problem scenario

Porcupine is walking on the beach on a warm, sunny day. The water is lapping at her feet, and she tries hard not to get her feet wet. Suddenly, she discovers a bottle washed up on the shore. She picks it up and looks inside. However, her little claws are too small to open it, so she asks one of the children for help. They can see a piece of paper with some writing on it.

They remove the paper and can see a message. It reads:

> *Help, it's Little Cactus and I am stranded on an island. There is no one around.*
> *I am lonely and would love someone to talk to.*

The educator or teacher, in character as Porcupine, asks the children:

- What can we do?
- Will we send a message in return?
- Will we swim to the island to find Little Cactus?
- Will we find a boat to cross the seas?
- What should we pack for our adventure?

If they travel to the island or write a letter to Little Cactus, what strategies could they suggest Little Cactus use to cope with feeling lonely? What could make Little Cactus feel better? Maybe the children could research strategies and prepare a booklet of ideas to share.

Planning educator or teacher interactions to build wellbeing

The educator or teacher takes the role of Porcupine and, depending on the interactions, takes on different positions in the play. In the under position, the educator or teacher asks the children about their experiences and elicits strategies. For example: What things have made you feel sad, angry, or worried in the past? How did you cope?

The educator or teacher adopts the above position when they ask the children to sort their coping responses as being helpful or non-helpful.

As the children and educator or teacher work together to put these in a book, they are in an equal position. The educator or teacher asks what coping skills worked for them in the past and what Little Cactus could try.

Take away messages

It is best to think of coping strategies as helpful or unhelpful rather than good or bad. All coping strategies serve a purpose, even if they are less productive. We can also improve our coping by drawing on past experiences. Thinking about how we have coped in the past can be one way we can improve our coping in the future.

Adventures for going deeper

In this Conceptual PlayWorld for Wellbeing, you and your children went on an adventure to the ocean through a magic portal. To bring more thinking about the concept and imagination to the journey, try this second adventure with a new problem where you explore appreciation and gratitude.

After being helped by his friends to learn coping skills for being lonely and his other emotions, Little Cactus feels particularly thankful and appreciates his animal friends for all their help. He had the idea to write a letter to his friends to explain how thankful he is for all their help, but now that he has sat down to write it, he does not know what to do!

Ask the children if they have ever written an appreciation letter or a thank-you note to someone before. If the children have, the educator or teacher should pretend to be Little Cactus writing the letter to friends. If not, the educator or teacher can help guide the students as if they were a peer advising Little Cactus. Provide children with paper and writing utensils, as necessary, to make their own demonstration cards. Prompt conversation throughout the creative process about the critical components of writing an appreciation or thank-you card.

Key Components to Guide the Children in

- Who are they writing their letter to? Why are they writing to that person?
- What should the note/letter/card look like?
- Should there be drawings or illustrations? Should there be an opening and closing (for example, "Dear _____," "From, _____.")?
- What should the note/letter/card say? What types of kind words go in an appreciation letter? What would make the other person happy or feel good when they read the letter?
- How would the children feel if they received a letter like this?

Chapter twelve

WORKING TOGETHER FOR MORE THAN JUST TREASURE

Introduction

Little Cactus has found a map to a treasure chest. But it is a long, challenging journey to find it, and the chest is sealed shut with a spell that can only be broken with the sound of music. Can Little Cactus and his animal friends work together and reap the rewards?

Wellbeing theme: Belonging and Inclusion

Learning Objectives

1. Children learn basic skills of collaboration and working together.
2. Children have opportunities to practice inclusive behaviours.

Designing a Conceptual PlayWorld for Wellbeing space

An area in the preschool is turned into treasure island. Designate the different stages of the journey: a desert, mountain, ocean, and cave. In the centre of a cave lies a treasure chest surrounded by musical instruments. Educators or teachers can prepare a map to find the secret treasure.

Entering and exiting the Conceptual PlayWorld for Wellbeing space

The educator or teacher (as Little Cactus) discovers a map and invites the children to look at all the steps of their journey. Everyone lines up according to their character and sets off

DOI: 10.4324/9781003206569-12

singing "We go marching one by one" to the tune of the "Marching Ants." The end lines can be adapted, for example:

- Little Cactus spikes his thumb

- And we go marching on and on

- To find that treasure chest.

 ## *Planning the play inquiry or problem scenario*

The treasure chest is in a cave that is hard to reach. Little Cactus and his friends must work together to reach it. They will need to use everybody's skills to get there.

Every time you get to an obstacle or a challenge in the adventure, have one of the characters use their unique skills to solve a problem for the group. When the obstacle is overcome, set off again and sing the song.

As you go, some of the friends might fear different things. Little Cactus might be afraid of crossing the river, for example. Can Porcupine (who is a good swimmer) help him?

Finally, they get to the treasure chest. Musical instruments surround it. The instruments say, "Play me to open the chest and break the magic spell."

Each group of characters sings a song and plays their music.

> We went marching one by one, hoorah! Hoorah!
> We went marching one by one, hoorah! Hoorah!
> Working together, we found the chest
> And now play music to open it
> To reveal the amazing treasure inside!

The educator or teacher, as Little Cactus, says, "It does not work. It is not loud enough. Maybe we need to all play together?" The children all sing the marching song and play their instruments.

The chest opens. It is full of treasure and a message from Wise Owl: "Congratulations! By using everybody's skills and working together, you not only overcame all the obstacles on your journey, but you were also able to open the chest. Enjoy the treasure, everybody! You have earned it."

After playing with the treasure, Little Cactus says it is time to go home. However, it is so far, and everyone is exhausted. He then reveals that he found another magic spell in the treasure chest – one to get them all back home in a heartbeat. All they must do is jump.

One-two-three: they jump and return as themselves.

Planning educator or teacher interactions to build wellbeing

The educator or teacher takes the above position to point out all the special skills of each animal and prompts discussions about what the children think of their own special skills. They lead the song and the musical challenge and ask the children if they all contributed to breaking the spell.

When the group gets through the challenge, the teacher or educator can observe how lucky they are to have friends who are good at different things. Everybody contributes to the group in the equal position.

Take away messages

Everybody has different ideas, looks different, has different home experiences, and has different skills that they contribute to the group. It helps people feel included when that contribution is acknowledged. Amazing things can happen when we can contribute by working together and cooperating.

Adventures for going deeper

To bring more thinking about the concept and imagination to the journey, you and the children could play an obstacle course game that supports the development of collaboration and practicing inclusive behaviours and belonging. For example:

Provide students with multiple items, such as pillows, carpet dots, pieces of paper, or other flat items that can be stepped on. You should have at least as many items as there are children, plus one (the more items, the easier the activity). Determine an area for the activity (the larger the space, the more challenging the activity) and mark it off using sidewalk chalk, string, jump ropes, or similar items that can make an appropriate and visible line.

Have all the children begin behind one line of the area and tell them their task for the activity is to use the provided objects to cross the activity area in front of them without stepping on the ground. If one student touches the ground, the entire group must pick up the items and start over, even if someone has made it to the end. The goal is to get every child across the space and the team does not win until every child is across.

This activity can be repeated by changing the parameters slightly to make it more challenging as children become better at working together. This may include taking away a large or heavily relied-on object, telling students they must all step across the ending line simultaneously, or taking all the items with them across the line. Timing how long it takes to move from one side to the other is optional.

Chapter thirteen

SNEEZING AND WHEEZING

Staying Connected

Introduction

Ahhhhhhhh Chooo! Porcupine wakes up one morning and she can't stop sneezing. Every time she sneezes, her quills pop out. Poor Porcupine must stay home and isolate to keep her friends safe, but can those friends help her stay connected?

Wellbeing theme: Belonging and Inclusion and Friendships

Learning Objectives

1. Children work together to find collective solutions.
2. Children practice and model inclusive behaviours that build a sense of belonging.
3. Children engage in scenarios that allow them to practice care and empathy towards others.

 Designing a Conceptual PlayWorld for Wellbeing space

Set up two signs that say: "Animal preschool" and "Porcupine Den" to show the different spaces. Create a tunnel for the porcupines to access their den. A rope creates two spaces, one for Porcupine's home and the animal preschool on the other.

DOI: 10.4324/9781003206569-13

Entering and exiting the Conceptual PlayWorld for Wellbeing space

Have the children decide which characters they would like to be. As they enter the room, have them walk into preschool like their characters: Snake, Deer, Eagle, Bat. You can have cousins, friends, and other family members as characters, such as the Deer family.

Planning the play inquiry or problem scenario

The children (in character) attend animal preschool and have free play until the educator or teacher (as Little Cactus) "calls the role" and notices that Porcupine is missing. Where could Porcupine be?

Then, there is a voicemail on the animal preschool phone:

> *This is Porcupine. I am very sad because I can't come to preschool because I am sick and need to stay at home in my den! I need to make sure nobody else catches what I have. But I will miss my friends. Can you find some ways to help me be with you, but keep you safe so you do not get sick?*

The children can then collectively think of ways to stay in touch with Porcupine and help her feel better. What helps them when they are feeling sad? The friends try out the different ways of staying in touch, and Porcupine gives feedback on what is working by sending back messages.

Planning educator or teacher interactions to build wellbeing

The educator or teacher in character as Little Cactus can call the roll, wonder where Porcupine is (under position), and introduce the problem scenario via voicemail (or pre-recorded message). The educator or teacher can also ask the children to brainstorm how they can communicate with Porcupine (above) and support the children in character to try different strategies. In the under position, the educator or teacher asks questions: How can they ensure Porcupine feels a part of their group? What are some things that might cheer her up? As Porcupine gets better, how will she know it is safe for her to return to preschool? Will there be a doctor that helps her or a particular test?

Take away messages

Since the worldwide emergence of COVID-19, the way we connect to and care for others has changed. There was a time when children would come to preschool with coughs and runny noses. However, now, for the protection of other children, educators, and teachers, children who display cold or flu symptoms are asked to stay home until they feel better. Because of this, many children will experience disruption to their friendships, but this is also an opportunity for children to engage in activities that show care and empathy. Even when apart, children can build friendships.

Adventures for going deeper

In this Conceptual PlayWorld for Wellbeing, you and your children went on an adventure to help Porcupine feel connected to her friends. To bring more thinking about the concept and imagination to the journey, you and the children could follow Little Cactus' example from the story and list all the things to be grateful for. He focused on the things that were going well. Using this strategy is integral to helping young children reframe their thoughts when things are not going their way.

They may be sick. Their friend might be away from preschool. They may miss out on a turn, lose a game, or feel like they are missing out on something – like when it is someone else's birthday. Reframing thinking to focus on what is going well can help children appreciate their circumstances. This activity could be done in pairs or a large group. Children can take turns expressing their feelings of gratitude. Some classes may start each day with a reflection of this type.

Children who have found themselves at home, perhaps unwell, might like to try out journaling.

To Make Journals

Provide students with many sheets of plain white paper and ensure they have help folding them in half horizontally. The folded papers should look something like a book with one creased edge. Using a stapler, push two to three staples into the crease to hold the pages together. The book may need to be opened and closed several times for it to stay open to specific pages.

On the book's front cover, students can write their names and decorate the booklet to their liking with colourful paints, crayons, stickers, glued photos, et cetera. On the top of and halfway down each following page, help the student write "Today I felt . . ." Each day, students can reflect for at least one minute about the things they felt throughout the day. They can choose one emotion and draw it within the journal for that day.

Chapter fourteen

RELAXING IN THE SNOW

Introduction

Oh dear! The weather has changed and suddenly it has snowed in the desert! Will Little Cactus and his friends make time for some fun before the snow melts? Or will worry take over and they all miss out?

Wellbeing theme: Relaxation and Coping

Learning Objectives

1. Children experience a brief mindfulness activity.
2. Children consider different ways we can respond to situations outside our control.
3. Children consider the role relaxation plays in coping.

Designing a Conceptual PlayWorld for Wellbeing space

A white blanket draped over a space in the preschool room simulates snow. A cardboard box is turned into a snowmobile, and it is located nearby. On the side of the snowmobile are the words "3-minute entry".

Entering and exiting the Conceptual PlayWorld for Wellbeing space

To enter the Conceptual PlayWorld for Wellbeing, the children go into the snowmobile.

Planning the play inquiry or problem scenario

The desert has turned into a snowfield. The children will dress warmly and go exploring in a snowmobile. They notice footprints and wade through the snow to see where they lead. They

DOI: 10.4324/9781003206569-14

discover Little Cactus, who is wearing an oversized jacket and feeling upset. In the snow is a message:

> *Help me. I woke up this morning and everything had changed. It was so cold and*
> *there was snow everywhere. I put on a jacket, so I didn't freeze, but I feel so upset*
> *and stressed.*
> *I do not know why my desert has become a snowfield.*

Allow a lot of excited chatter and different scenarios to come from the children. What can they do? They take Little Cactus and return to the snowmobile, comforting him. When the children turn the radio sound system on (mobile phone with a recording), they hear an important clue:

> *"Good morning, everyone. When you are worried or stressed you can try a three-*
> *minute body scan meditation to help you calm down."*

But what does that mean? How do we do that? The children see a series of arrows pointing to the Meditation Centre.

The children visit the Centre and meet Wise Owl (the educator or teacher in character), who can guide them in a simple body scan.

- Start with the children lying down, closing their eyes, and listening to the snow falling.

- Encourage them to imagine the weight of their bodies lying on a big cosy bed and to breathe slowly.

- Have them take three deep breaths and slowly exhale as though they are moving snowflakes.

- Guide them to scan through their body and notice the different parts. Start with the feet, legs, and stomach. Can they feel their heart beating?

- Can they feel their hands being heavy, then relax their arms and soften their shoulders?

- Have them notice their neck and throat, then relax their faces.

- Ask them to notice how their whole body is feeling. When they are ready, have them take a deep breath and open their eyes.

How is everybody feeling? What would you want to do if you found a big snowfield around your house?

Planning educator or teacher interactions to build wellbeing

As a character in the story, the educator or teacher can introduce the scenario that the desert has turned into a snowfield, and they have a snowmobile to help them explore. The educator or teacher can also notice the footprints (equal position) and ask for help from the children to read the message and follow the signs to the Meditation Centre (under position). At the Centre, the educator or teacher can take on the role of Wise Owl and guide the children in a body scan (above). Then, they can encourage the children to notice if they feel better (under position), and to think about fun ways to respond to the snow. They all go outside and play. Little Cactus is feeling much better and happier.

Exit the Conceptual PlayWorld as the sun goes down on the snowmobile.

Take away messages

Rapid changes in weather patterns and uncertainty around global events mean that young children face regular uncertainty and unpredictability. Such changes may also impact the daily lives of their families. Teaching children relaxation strategies is one way children can cope when they feel that challenges are beyond their control. Relaxation strategies form an important aspect of emotional regulation. Just as children have different preferences for colours or activities, their preferences for what helps them relax also vary. Exposing children to various methods helps them identify what works best for them.

Adventures for going deeper

In this Conceptual PlayWorld for Wellbeing, you and your children went on an adventure to the snow and learned how to relax when something unexpected happens. To bring more thinking about the concept and imagination to the journey, you and the children could research the role relaxation plays in coping as follows:

As Little Cactus explores the desert with his friends, he may encounter new challenges or difficulties in getting around. Sometimes, Little Cactus must learn to take on new ways to help solve problems and learn about new friends. The best way to cope with situations is when we are relaxed. Yoga is a relaxation strategy that children can try.

While optionally playing quiet meditative music or even ambient desert sounds, have the educator or teacher lead students in a calming yoga activity. The educator or teacher should demonstrate each pose before asking the students to attempt the pose. The educator or teacher should remind students that none of the poses are required and that some may be too difficult for them without practice, but that the important part of the activity is trying their best and focusing on feeling relaxed, calm, and in tune with their bodies. Students should be allowed to modify poses for their own physical comfort and ability.

Tree pose – "The Little Cactus" pose

Pose Description: Stand with feet flat on the floor, shoulder-width apart. Raise your arms simultaneously from your side, elbows down and palm up, like branches of a cactus, until they are roughly as high as your shoulders. Your arms should curve up at the elbow to make a u-shape. If you have the balance, raise one foot off the ground and place the bottom of your foot against the side of your opposite leg, holding it there.

Warrior I pose – "Towards the sun pose"

Pose Description: Start standing with both feet on the floor with your arms at your sides. Step forward with your right foot until your hips stretch, and you lean forward to even out weight between the two legs. Bend your front knee so that you are lunging forward, and your back leg straightens. Turn your left heel so that it is perpendicular with your right foot (turnabout 45°). Raise your arms straight up from each shoulder towards the ceiling. Hold this pose for a good stretch. You can repeat this by lunging with the left foot forward for more of a stretch.

Warrior II pose – "Bat pose"

Pose Description: Start standing with both feet on the floor with your arms at your sides. Step to the side so that your feet are slightly wider than shoulder width apart and stretch your arms out to the sides to make a straight line across your shoulders. Turn one foot out approximately 90° so that it is perpendicular with the other foot. Lunge and place your knee above your ankle. Turn your head to look over your bent knee. You can repeat this by lunging with your other leg for more of a stretch.

Cobra pose – "Desert Snake pose"

Pose Description: Lie down on the floor flat on your stomach. Place your hands palm down on the floor directly underneath your shoulders. Bend your elbows back and keep them close to your sides. Lift your chest slowly off the floor and roll your shoulders back to keep your stomach against the floor. Keep your elbows close to your body and hold for a stretch.

Corpse pose – "Laying in the sand pose"

Pose Description: Lay flat on your back on the floor, with legs spread comfortably and slightly apart. Your arms should lay out at your sides, at least a few inches from your body, palms up.

Chapter fifteen

THE TWINKLE PARTY

Introduction

Bat has exciting news: for one night, the Glow Worms are hosting a Twinkle Party at The Big Cave. However, she has lost her voice, and her friends are not paying attention. Can the group band together and help Bat communicate?

Wellbeing theme: Friendship

Learning Objectives

1. Children learn listening skills that can be used with peers.
2. Children learn that listening to others can facilitate care and empathy.

 ## *Designing a Conceptual PlayWorld for Wellbeing space*

You will need two spaces: an animal Friends Park where the children will meet in character and The Big Cave, with tinkling lights (maybe a disco ball) and a speaker for music.

 ## *Entering and exiting the Conceptual PlayWorld for Wellbeing space*

The children enter and exit the Conceptual PlayWorld for Wellbeing through a door that has three signs with arrows. One says "Friend's Park", one says "Children's preschool", and third says "The Big Cave."

 ## *Planning the play inquiry or problem scenario*

Bat is excited and worried. The Glow Worms put her in charge of inviting everyone to come to the Twinkle Party at The Big Cave. It is being held tonight! However, when she goes to

DOI: 10.4324/9781003206569-15

Friends Park to tell her friends, she discovers she has lost her voice. How can she tell her friends?

Everybody is talking so loudly that they overlook Bat. She gets sad. The educator or teacher (in character) notices and figures out Bat has lost her voice but has something important to say.

The other animals might realise they have not been good listening friends. How can they help Bat communicate if she cannot speak? Some strategies might include learning sign language, doing charades, drawing a picture, or writing a letter.

The children head back to their classroom to brainstorm and research ways that Bat might share a message without talking.

When they return to the Conceptual PlayWorld for Wellbeing, they try out the different strategies. They need to be patient while they decipher Bat's message. Finally, when they figure it out, they can all head off to The Big Cave for the Twinkle Party.

The Big Cave lights up. The educator or teacher could kick off the party with the "Glow Worm" song by Bing Crosby or the Mills Brothers. Bat's voice could even return in time to read the poem (try using a small bongo drum as a prop): "I wish I were a glow worm; A glow worm's never glum; 'Cause how can you be grumpy, when the sun shines out your. . . [*pause*] tail?"

Planning educator or teacher interactions to build wellbeing

The class separates into characters, and they enter the Conceptual PlayWorld for Wellbeing. The educator or teacher pulls aside the bats and says they have lost their voice but need to invite their friends to the party. Let the play unfold. The educator or teacher can then draw the group's attention to notice Bat's problem, link the listening skill to friendship, and wonder about different ways to communicate (under position).

In the classroom, guide the group to find solutions and maybe learn some sign language (above position). Back at Friends Park, support the children to guess what Bat is saying. The educator or teacher could also take the role of Bat for reading the poem (above position).

Take away messages

Listening skills can be tricky for young children. While they might listen well in a class context (or show signs of developing that skill), the skill of listening to friends can take time. In this Conceptual PlayWorld for Wellbeing, children have an opportunity to practice listening. Through rehearsal and practicing, most children will learn the vital friendship skill of listening.

Adventures for going deeper

To bring more thinking about the concept and imagination to the journey, you and the children could divide students into pairs for this activity and tell them that they will be practicing being good listeners to friends.

Ask all students to think about a topic that makes them excited and that they could talk about to a friend. Pick one student to be the "speaker" first and have the other be the "listener". Tell students that the "speaker" will have one minute to discuss their chosen topic. However, during this time, the "listener" should be as bad of a listener as they can be to their friend, no matter how interesting they think the topic might be. You may need to tell students that there are parameters to how "badly" they can listen (for example, no screaming or yelling, no walking away).

Set a timer for one minute and have students follow your instructions. When the minute is over, tell students to try the exercise again, but with the "listener" instead choosing to use their best listening skills. Repeat both versions of the activity with the "listener" and "speaker" switching roles. After the exercise has been completed, bring the students together for a discussion. Ask them what it looked like when someone was being a lousy listener. How were they behaving? What was different when they were a good listener? Ask students to compare their feelings as the speaker when their friend was being a good vs lousy listener. How did it feel?

Chapter sixteen

AN ACORN FEAST FOR DEER

Introduction

Deer has discovered a pile of acorns at the centre of a complicated maze. However, she finds the challenge too hard. Bat encourages Deer to think more positively. Will Deer be able to reach her favourite food?

Wellbeing theme: Coping

Learning Objectives

1. Children identify helpful and unhelpful self-talk.
2. Children learn that thoughts can influence feelings and behaviour.
3. Children practice encouraging statements for others.

 ### *Designing a Conceptual PlayWorld for Wellbeing space*

Create a maze with ropes or cardboard boxes with something special in the centre that can represent acorns. This becomes the Conceptual PlayWorld for Wellbeing space.

 ### *Entering and exiting the Conceptual PlayWorld for Wellbeing space*

Children put on deer antlers and enter the maze. They may make the antlers themselves, or they can be pre-prepared by the teacher or educator. Sun hats (plus some imagination) can be a quick solution to creating antlers.

When they have finished their journey, they take their antlers off.

DOI: 10.4324/9781003206569-16

Planning the play inquiry or problem scenario

Deer and Bat come to the maze and find a note:

> *Dear Deer, we have left a big pile of acorns for you at the centre of this maze. We know they are your favourite. Love, the Chipmunks.*

Deer reads the message and starts off, but immediately becomes disheartened and complains. "It is too hard! I will never find the way! It is so far!"

Bat notices. "Deer! Those kinds of words will not help you. It would be best if you said positive things to yourself to reach the acorns."

Deer says she cannot think of any positive things to say and gives up. Bat follows Deer, and they exit the Conceptual PlayWorld – taking off her antlers.

Together, the class brainstorms a list of positive words and thoughts that might help Deer. They can create a list with examples like:

"Sometimes things can be hard, but they can get easier when we try."
"Giving up means missing out."
"It might feel hard, but I can do it."

Enter back into the Conceptual PlayWorld as Deer and a number of children playing Bat. The Bats take one sticker each and put it in the maze. As Deer passes a yellow sticker, the Bats shout out: "You are adventurous!" And the Deer replies, "Yes! I am adventurous. I can find the acorns."

Eventually, Deer reaches the centre of the maze and eats the delicious acorns while the Bats cheer her on.

Planning educator or teacher interactions to build wellbeing

The educator or teacher – in either character or as Wise Owl – can support the children to read the message at the beginning, prompt Deer to complain as much as they can, and ask the Bats if they think the negative thoughts will help (above position). Guide the children to think about what might help instead (equal position).

While creating the list of positive thoughts, the educator or teacher can reflect on how our thoughts and words can change the way we act and change the way we feel (equal position). They can make us feel sad and like we want to give up, or they can make us feel motivated and full of energy.

You can also help the children reflect on the question: Is it easier to think of good ways to support your friends than good thoughts to encourage yourself?

Back in the maze in character, the educator or teacher can model encouraging and positive thoughts (above position).

Take away messages

The thoughts and words we use to talk to ourselves can influence how we feel and act. Our thinking can be helpful sometimes. We can help ourselves to think more helpfully if we try to talk to ourselves as well as we would talk to a best friend or our favourite person. Our thinking can be powerful and help us do amazing things if we can be kind to ourselves.

Adventures for going deeper

To bring more thinking about the concept and imagination to the journey, you and the children could take the opportunity to explore further their thinking and feelings and how their thoughts and feelings can be related. Furthermore, how their thinking can be different from their peers.

Tell children they will put different events or experiences into different categories of feelings.

Remind students that different experiences might bring about different emotions for different people. What is an exciting experience for one child might be boring or scary for another.

Tell them that there are no wrong answers, only answers that are right for themselves. Provide students with a blank piece of paper (or pre-make the templates for categorising yourself). Have students draw four straight lines across the page horizontally ("side-to-side" may be the best direction for kids). Have them draw five evenly spaced lines across the page vertically ("top-to-bottom" may be the best direction for kids). In the top row, help students draw a feeling related to a list of events or situations that the educator or teacher will read out, one at a time. Example Events List: Dropping your ice cream, getting a gift you did not expect from a friend, speaking in front of a crowd of people, meeting a new friend on the playground, getting ready to go to the doctors, and so on.

A more advanced step is to ask children to retell how they might think and feel at the time to show that our thoughts can influence how we feel. Comparing children's thoughts and feelings can highlight how some thoughts can be more helpful than others. For instance, an unhelpful thought to dropping an ice cream might be: "I will never eat ice cream again!" A thought like this might make someone feel very sad. A more helpful thought could be, "I will be able to have another ice cream next time, or worse things could happen."

Chapter seventeen

HELPING EAGLE FLY AGAIN

Introduction

Eagle is feeling so sad she does not even want to fly up to her nest. It was her birthday last week. The party was so much fun, but now she feels she has nothing to celebrate. Snake asks Eagle to remember all the best moments. Does that help Eagle feel better? Will she fly again?

Wellbeing theme: Positive emotions

Learning Objectives

1. Children learn about savouring positive emotions.

 ## *Designing a Conceptual PlayWorld for Wellbeing space*

Create a green meadow in a forest where Eagle can sit, then create Eagle's Nest high up in a tree where they can go to fly. A fort or climbing frame would work well for this space.

 ## *Entering and exiting the Conceptual PlayWorld for Wellbeing space*

Ask the group to choose an animal character from the story: Porcupine, Deer, Snake, Bat, or Eagle. Design two big "trees" for them to enter, and they can fly, slither, walk, or waddle into the forest.

 ## *Planning the play inquiry or problem scenario*

After the children have played in the forest as their animals, ask them to go to the green meadow. That is when the group discovers that Eagle is really sad.

But why? Eagle explains it was her birthday last week; she remembers it was so much fun, but now she feels like there is nothing to celebrate. How can she feel better?

DOI: 10.4324/9781003206569-17

The group can offer suggestions. Then the educator or teacher (in character) can suggest remembering all the best moments of her party. Will that help? Maybe. Let us investigate that!

The children can then exit the Conceptual PlayWorld for Wellbeing and be led in an activity where they can draw or paint a happy memory.

Later, the children – in character – can return to the forest meadow with their work and share it in a circle. Finally, they come to Eagle, who shares all the good moments from her birthday. She feels happy again and flies off to Eagle's Nest to hang up her picture.

Eagle invites all her friends to join her up there and hang their pictures on the nest. Then it is time to exit the Conceptual PlayWorld filled with good memories.

Planning educator or teacher interactions to build wellbeing

The educator or teacher (in character) can provide insights and prompts to the children – guiding them to the meadow, noticing Eagle is sad, and guiding the conversation about solutions.

The educator/teacher can also suggest that when they are sad, sometimes it helps to remember happy moments.

In the classroom, the educator or teacher in the above position can explain the idea of savouring: when we remember and recall a favourable event. It works best if we remember lots of details. As the children make their drawings, try to draw out specific details.

Back in the forest, the educator or teacher can take the role of Eagle, with their own picture and details of the party. Then they can fly away to Eagle's Nest and invite all the children to join them and hang their pictures.

Take away messages

Different experiences and activities can lead to positive emotions. Because of this, children might have favourite events such as birthday celebrations or traditions with their family that conjure up positive feelings and good memories. Something as simple as the taste of chocolate or the excitement of going to the movies could be experiences children can savour and cherish. Savouring allows children to extend the positive emotions that might coincide with a favourite memory.

Adventures for going deeper

To bring more thinking about the concept and imagination to the journey, talk to the children about how shooting stars do not happen all the time and are not always in the sky, but are something that you can look forward to, appreciate, and savour when you do see them. Then, ask children to reflect on what events or activities do not happen all the time but make them happy. Do they appreciate those things more because they are things that happen rarely? Do they think back on those memories and savour them?

Hang up a large blue or black piece of construction paper on a wall, on the floor, or over a window – completely blank with nothing on it. Explain to students that this represents the night sky in the desert and ask them what might be missing. Prompt them answer the stars in the sky, if necessary. Provide students with a blank shooting star outline. They can either cut them out themselves or you can have them pre-cut for time. Ask the students to brainstorm at least three rare activities or events they want to savour and have them write or draw them onto the shooting star. Then, help them glue or tape the shooting stars to the construction paper mat, creating a night sky of things to appreciate and savour.

Chapter eighteen

BREATHING BUDDIES

Introduction

Little Cactus and his friends decide to visit cousins in another valley, but after crossing the desert and walking through Spider Swamp, they are too tired to get over Big Mountain. They decide to use hot air balloons instead. Can they stay relaxed enough to stay steady and safe in the hot air balloon?

Wellbeing theme: Relaxation

Learning Objectives

1. Children learn about deep breathing.
2. Children practice deep breathing exercises to build into a relaxation skill repertoire.

 Designing a Conceptual PlayWorld for Wellbeing space

Create as few or as many challenges as you want for the adventure. Use a rough drawing of a mountain on the wall and boxes to designate the hot air balloons.

Create a map showing the route they need to follow.

 Entering and exiting the Conceptual PlayWorld for Wellbeing space

After children choose their characters, load up their pretend backpacks, blow a whistle, and the group can set off.

DOI: 10.4324/9781003206569-18

Planning the play inquiry or problem scenario

The children receive an invitation from their cousins to visit them in the other valley. Included is a map and a list of equipment they will need.

As they enter the Conceptual PlayWorld for Wellbeing as a group and with all the equipment they need, they can start to navigate a series of obstacles on the map. Encourage the children to get through the obstacles using the equipment they packed. After lots of play and fun, the children arrive at Big Mountain.

"Oh no! We are all too tired, even Eagle and Bat. How will everybody get across?" Talk about different strategies, then notice a box near the Big Mountain. The box has a note.

> *To Little Cactus and his friends,*
> *Big Mountain is very dangerous to cross, especially when you are tired. I have left these hot air balloons for you. You will need to blow them up with big, slow, deep breaths. When you are flying, you will need to stay very relaxed so the balloon keeps working.*
> *Love, Wise Owl.*

Have the students notice that when they take big, slow breaths they can feel calmer. As you start to fly, some of the characters might get nervous. Encourage them to take big, slow breaths to stay relaxed and calm.

The children slowly and gently float over the mountains, descend into the valley, and meet up with their cousins.

After the play is finished, the children can float back home while staying very relaxed. Once landed, the children can jump out of the hot air balloons and unpack their backpacks. The educator or teacher can blow the whistle to signify the end of play.

Planning educator or teacher interactions to build wellbeing

The educator or teacher helps read the map (equal position), prompts the children to use their equipment, and helps read the note.

The teacher or educator in the above position can also remind the children that we can take big deep breaths that make our stomachs blow out, which helps us calm down. However, taking tiny, quick breaths does not help us feel relaxed. Children can consider the difference between the two breathing types and what is more effective for them.

Take away messages

While breathing comes naturally for nearly everyone, as a tool for relaxation, many people can breathe too quickly or too shallowly. In this Conceptual PlayWorld for Wellbeing, educators, teachers, and children in the early years can experience the importance of deep slow breaths as a coping strategy that they may choose to try out again when they face a worry or challenge.

Adventures for going deeper

To bring more thinking about the concept and imagination to the journey, begin a new activity by asking children to sit quietly and breathe normally. Ask them to pay attention to their breathing and ask if they notice anything about it. How does their body move? How does it feel to pay attention to their breathing? Then have the students lie down on their backs on the floor.

Have them count to ten, slowly, or count for them after instructing children to try and relax their bodies and muscles as much as possible. Have children place their hands on their stomachs, palms down. Instruct children to breathe in through their nose for four seconds, then to hold their breath for four seconds.

Tell children to breathe out slowly until all the air is gone. Have children repeat this process until they focus on their breath and slowly relax. You can help children with timing by counting aloud for them, if necessary, demonstrating yourself, and counting silently on your fingers as you breathe.

Chapter nineteen

CELEBRATION OF STRENGTHS

Introduction

Little Cactus had a challenging week. His prickles caused so many problems and now he wishes he was a smooth-skinned cactus instead. So, while Deer is building her new house, Little Cactus thinks he will only cause more problems. Will the children be able to prove him wrong?

Wellbeing theme: Belonging and Inclusion

Learning Objectives

1. Children learn to focus on individual strengths and the benefits of using them.
2. Children identify their own strengths.
3. Children consider how using strengths can make them feel good about themselves and happier.

 ## *Designing a Conceptual PlayWorld for Wellbeing space*

You will need to designate or create a forest environment for this Conceptual PlayWorld for Wellbeing. Hide some forest animal faces around the room, including several wolves. Create a forest post office box.

Prepare materials that children can use to build a house for Deer. Have some PlayDoh and lots and lots of toothpicks (Little Cactus' spikes) on hand.

 ## *Entering and exiting the Conceptual PlayWorld for Wellbeing space*

The children enter and exit the forest through a door with two big trees on either side and a sign saying, "This way to Deer Forest."

DOI: 10.4324/9781003206569-19

Planning the play inquiry or problem scenario

The children are going to play in the forest. When they enter, they need to find all the different animals. When they find an animal, a child can put their mask on and pretend to be that animal.

During the play, announce that the *Forest Post* has arrived. Inside is a letter from Little Cactus.

> *Dear Friends,*
>
> *I have had a terrible week. On Monday, I accidentally spiked a friendly bird who dropped by for a chat. On Tuesday, a little girl walked past and I popped her balloon. On Wednesday, Squirrel gave me a high-five, and I made him bleed. On Thursday, I popped a bike tyre. I wish I didn't have these stupid spikes and had smooth skin instead.*
>
> *Now, to make matters worse, Deer has invited me to help build her house with our friends, but I am sure my spikes will be a big problem. I don't want to go. Can you think of any reasons why I should go? Love, Little Cactus*

The children can then leave the Conceptual PlayWorld and design a house for Deer. Brainstorm all the different ways Little Cactus' spikes could be used. Some could include making a spiky trap to stop the wolves, making a brush or back scratcher for Deer, pinning up artwork in the new house, putting the spikes on the roof to stop the cheeky birds from stealing the roof for their nests, or even making a doormat to scrape off the mud.

Have the children write a letter to Little Cactus explaining how his spikes will actually make the house better. Encourage Little Cactus to come.

Then it's time to go back to the forest and build the house for Deer with Little Cactus. The educator or teacher (as Little Cactus) dispenses the spikes (toothpicks) and is amazed at how clever the children are for the way they have incorporated their designs.

Little Cactus can also observe how the children are using all their different strengths to build the house. Once the house is built, have the children test their design and play out the scenarios. Will it keep away the wolves? Will it stop the birds? Is it a good brush for Deer? Does it stop the mud?

Planning educator or teacher interactions to build wellbeing

A child as Little Cactus in the under position asks the other children to help build a house.

The educator or teacher takes the role of Deer to bring drama to the situation and reports to the children what they observe in the above position.

Little Cactus observes the strengths each of the individual children working together brought to the task and tells the children what they noticed (above). Was someone open to ideas? Was someone good at helping others to join in? Was someone showing good listening skills? What were the strengths that the children thought they brought into the activity? Little Cactus reports to Deer.

Deer, in the under position, asks the children to check the report, and the children, in the above position, add to the report and discuss what it says.

Take away messages

Identifying and noticing strengths in yourself and others can help create a positive environment for children to play and learn in. Using strengths and knowing our strengths can be critical to our wellbeing. Educators and teachers play an essential role in identifying strengths and helping children use them. This Conceptual PlayWorld for Wellbeing provides an opportunity for children to engage in an activity where strengths could be observed and pointed out.

Adventures for going deeper

To bring more thinking about the concept and imagination to the journey, you and the children could play games that support wellbeing through finding the strengths of oneself and others.

Divide students into small groups of three to five students per group whom they do not normally spend time with. Tell students that this activity aims to find one unique or special thing about each person in the group that is different from every other member of the group.

These may range from being a good older sister to being very good at gymnastics. Students should sit in a circle facing each other and go around the circle one at a time to share something about themselves.

Students are also encouraged to talk about these things between suggestions and to share things about one another. The goal of the activity is to recognise and appreciate how students may be different, so remind students, when necessary, that the unique things they share should be good and positive things about themselves.

Chapter twenty

A NEW FRIEND

Introduction

There is a new friend starting *Animal Kinder* (or Animal Nursery, Preschool) called Arlo. She is a hermit crab who is shy and nervous. How can the class be welcoming of their new friend?

Wellbeing theme: Friendships, Belonging, and Inclusion

Learning Objectives

1. Children have an opportunity to practice meeting new friends and making them feel welcome.
2. Children can consider what it might feel like to be in a new setting.
3. Children will practice making others feel included.

 ### *Designing a Conceptual PlayWorld for Wellbeing space*

Prepare animal masks that the children can use. There will be three zones for games the animals can choose to play: The Floor is Lava, PlayDoh Creations, and the Building Block Construction Zone. For the final session, you will need a little box.

 ### *Entering and exiting the Conceptual PlayWorld for Wellbeing space*

Have children line up in a row in their animal character, ring a school bell, and announce it's time to go to Animal Kinder (or Animal Nursery, Preschool)!

DOI: 10.4324/9781003206569-20

Planning the play inquiry or problem scenario

Direct the children to play in any of the three zones. Have them rotate through each of the activities and have lots of fun.

As the children are settled into the play, play a doorbell sound and say, "Kinder (or Nursery, Preschool) Post is here." A letter from Little Cactus has arrived:

> *Dear children,*
>   *My good friend Arlo, the hermit crab, is starting Kinder (or Nursery, Preschool) today. Can you think of things that will help her feel welcome?*

Exit the Conceptual PlayWorld, and have the children sit in a circle and think about how Arlo might be feeling. How would they feel if they were also new? What are some strategies that they can think of to help her feel a part of the Kinder (or Nursery, Preschool)? You could create a visual representation of them.

Then have the children go back into the Conceptual PlayWorld and play the games. Arlo arrives, but the instructor should let the children know that Arlo is very shy. The educator or teacher, in character, can offer some reasoning or prompts about why.

Eventually, have the children try different strategies and discover Arlo loves to read and play in the sandpit. She even gets to choose the book for story time in the afternoon.

Planning educator or teacher interactions to build wellbeing

The educator or teacher in the above position can adopt the role of Wise Owl and prompt the children to reflect on their own feelings when they navigate change. Have you ever started anywhere new? How did you feel? Did it take time for you to feel comfortable? What did your friends, educators, or teachers do to help you feel comfortable?

They can observe in the under position and then guide the children as they implement their strategies and ideas (equal position). Another educator or teacher can also take on the role of Arlo, being shy and hiding away.

Take away messages

Starting somewhere new can feel uncomfortable or awkward. Some children might feel nervous or anxious. Starting or returning to preschool after a break, starting a new hobby, or joining a new group can require children to take time to readjust. In this Conceptual PlayWorld for Wellbeing, we explore the role other children can play in helping children transition and feel more comfortable. This activity emphasises that all children have a role to play in helping other children feel included and like they belong.

Adventures for going deeper

This Conceptual PlayWorld can extend over multiple days as the children brainstorm strategies to help someone feel welcome and discuss how to implement them – and then reflect on their strategies.

There are a range of additional wellbeing activities you can do to facilitate conversation and learning outside of the Conceptual PlayWorld, like playing Feelings Charades, where children take turns acting out a different emotion they draw from a bowl and then the class guesses what it is.

You can also ask the children to work together to come up with a list of things to say to a new friend, and then share it with everybody. That list could become a part of your learning space.

Another step is to have the children work in groups of two or three and give them a scenario where they might meet somebody new – they meet at a park, the first day of school, or at a party. They can take turns introducing themselves. Between each practice round, ask students to share what they said and how they thought it went.

Chapter twenty-one

COMPLIMENTS UNLOCKED

Introduction

The butterflies are holding their annual *Compliment Olympics*, but strong winds are keeping the competitors away. Can the animal friends participate instead?

Wellbeing theme: Friendship

Learning Objectives

1. Children will learn that there are different types of compliments and focusing on skills and attributes can be more rewarding than focusing on appearances.

 ## *Designing a Conceptual PlayWorld for Wellbeing space*

Designate an area that will become Little Cactus' house and create an area that becomes the site of the Complement Olympics. Use a toy or object to be Pigeon and tie a message to his foot. The message says:

> *Dear Children,*
> *The butterflies are holding their annual Compliment Olympics, but strong winds are keeping the competitors away. Without your help we won't be able to create our 'Kaleidoscope of Compliments.' Can you compete instead?*
> *Love, Queen Butterfly*
> *PS. If you would like to compete, create a butterfly and write your best compliment on the back of it. Then float to our Olympics on this magic string the Spider Queen sent me.*

Prepare materials for the children to create butterflies (paper, paint, and string). These will become a "Kaleidoscope of Compliments." You can hang it from a cord on the ceiling so it looks like they float.

DOI: 10.4324/9781003206569-21

Prepare "gold medals" for each child in the class.

You will also need a long piece of string.

 ## *Entering and exiting the Conceptual PlayWorld for Wellbeing space*

To visit Little Cactus' house in the desert, have the children stand at a door with a sign that says, "Cactus' House this way:.

To visit the Compliment Olympics, have the children put on their animal masks, hold a magic, invisible string, and float like balloons to your Olympics site.

Designing a Conceptual PlayWorld space

The friends are playing hide and seek at Little Cactus' house. Everybody is having lots of fun when they receive a message by Pigeon Post (a toy with a message tied to his leg).

The educator or teacher reads out the urgent message from Queen Butterfly. Can the children help?

Exit the Conceptual PlayWorld and prepare to take part in the Olympics.

The children will need to create butterflies that can hang or be pinned up with space on the back or around the edges to write a compliment. They can create more than one.

You can also have a circle-time session to talk about compliments and how it makes people feel good to receive them. You can ask the children to think of a time when they received one.

Then, as a class, think of different ways to give a compliment (steer them towards values and away from physical appearance) and make a list such as:

• You are a good reader.

• You are a great listener.

• You are fun to play with.

• You are good at building.

• Your paintings are so colourful.

• You were very kind to me when I was feeling upset the other day.

Then set a challenge for the whole class to think about good compliments about their classmates and write them on their butterflies.

The educator or teacher can ensure that every child has an equal number of compliments that will be part of the kaleidoscope.

Then enter the next Conceptual PlayWorld, float to the Olympics, and deliver the compliments. The Queen Butterfly can help each of the children read out their compliments. The children can then hang their compliments as part of the display.

She cannot decide who wins, so all the children receive a gold medal for being good at compliments.

Planning educator or teacher interactions to build wellbeing

The educator or teacher is an equal play partner in the first round and assists with reading out Pigeon's message. In the second round, the educator or teacher becomes Queen Butterfly. As Queen Butterfly, the educator or teacher can assist with reading the messages and can give out gold medals.

Take away messages

Children can learn ways to compliment other children and adults. They can also learn that some compliments are better than others. Focusing on providing compliments on things other children do or can do – things they are good at, things they have done – are better than compliments based on how someone looks (such as, "you are pretty").

Adventures for going deeper

Give students small pieces of paper or note cards to bring more thinking about the concept and imagination to the journey. Help students develop three to five positive statements about themselves and write one on each card or piece of paper. The educator or teacher may need to provide examples.

Have students keep the cards in a special place, like in their backpack, for times they may need reminders or a pick-me-up. Tell students they can look back on these cards during those times.

Students can be encouraged to decorate their cards with butterflies for extra creativity.

Example positive statement cards for children

"I am a kind friend."

"I do my best and that is enough."

"My mum/dad/parent/adult loves me."

"I am funny."

REFERENCE

Fleer, M. (2018). Conceptual playworlds: the role of imagination in play and learning. *Early Years*, *41*, 353–364. doi: 10.1080/09575146.2018.1549024.